CREATIVE HOMEOWNER® ULTIMATE GUIDE TO

Ceramic & Stone Tile

CREATIVE
HOMEOWNER®

ULTIMATE GUIDE TO

Ceramic & Stone Tile

SELECT · INSTALL · MAINTAIN

Ceramic · Stone · Glass
Mosaic · Porcelain

CREATIVE HOMEOWNER®, Upper Saddle River, New Jersey

CREATIVE HOMEOWNER®

A Division of Federal Marketing Corp.
Upper Saddle River, NJ

CERAMIC & STONE TILE
MANAGING EDITOR: Fran J. Donegan
SENIOR EDITOR: Mike McClintock
CONTRIBUTING EDITOR: Steve Willson
ASSOCIATE EDITOR: Paul Rieder
ASSISTANT EDITORS: Evan Lambert, Dan Lane
PROOFREADERS: Dan Houghtaling, Sharon Ranftle
PHOTO EDITORS: Robyn Poplasky, Stanley Sudol
TECHNICAL CONSULTANT: Robert Daniels, Executive Director, Tile Council of America, Inc.
LAYOUT & DESIGN: David Geer
ILLUSTRATIONS: Robert LaPointe
ART DEVELOPMENT: Glee Barre
PRINCIPAL PHOTOGRAPHER: John Parsekian
PHOTO ASSISTANTS: Dan Lane, Dan Houghtaling, James Parlagi

CREATIVE HOMEOWNER
VP/PUBLISHER: Brian Toolan
VP/EDITORIAL DIRECTOR: Timothy O. Bakke
PRODUCTION MANAGER: Kimberly H. Vivas
MANAGING EDITOR: Fran J. Donegan
ART DIRECTOR: David Geer

Manufactured in China

Current Printing (last digit)
10 9 8 7 6 5 4 3 2

Ceramic & Stone Tile
First published as *Ceramic Tile*
Library of Congress Control Number: 2005908264
ISBN-10: 1-58011-297-8
ISBN-13: 978-1-58011-297-0

CREATIVE HOMEOWNER®
A Division of Federal Marketing Corp.
24 Park Way, Upper Saddle River, NJ 07458
www.creativehomeowner.com

Metric Equivalents

Length

1 inch	25.4mm
1 foot	0.3048m
1 yard	0.9144m
1 mile	1.61km

Area

1 square inch	645mm^2
1 square foot	0.0929m^2
1 square yard	0.8361m^2
1 acre	4046.86m^2
1 square mile	2.59km^2

Volume

1 cubic inch	16.3870cm^3
1 cubic foot	0.03m^3
1 cubic yard	0.77m^3

Common Lumber Equivalents

Sizes: Metric cross sections are so close to their U.S. sizes, as noted below, that for most purposes they may be considered equivalents.

Dimensional lumber	1 × 2	19 × 38mm
	1 × 4	19 × 89mm
	2 × 2	38 × 38mm
	2 × 4	38 × 89mm
	2 × 6	38 × 140mm
	2 × 8	38 × 184mm
	2 × 10	38 × 235mm
	2 × 12	38 × 286mm
Sheet sizes	4 × 8 ft.	1200 × 2400mm
	4 × 10 ft.	1200 × 3000mm
Sheet thicknesses	¼ in.	6mm
	⅜ in.	9mm
	½ in.	12mm
	¾ in.	19mm
Stud/joist spacing	16 in. o.c.	400mm o.c.
	24 in. o.c.	600mm o.c.

Capacity

1 fluid ounce	29.57mL
1 pint	473.18mL
1 quart	0.95L
1 gallon	3.79L

Weight

1 ounce	28.35g
1 pound	0.45kg

Temperature

Fahrenheit = Celsius × 1.8 + 32
Celsius = Fahrenheit − 32 × 5⁄9

Nail Size & Length

Penny Size	Nail Length
2d	1"
3d	1¼"
4d	1½"
5d	1¾"
6d	2"
7d	2¼"
8d	2½"
9d	2¾"
10d	3"
12d	3¼"
16d	3½"

SAFETY

Although the methods in this book have been reviewed for safety, it is not possible to overstate the importance of using the safest methods you can. What follows are reminders—some do's and don'ts of work safety—to use along with your common sense.

- *Always* use caution, care, and good judgment when following the procedures described in this book.

- *Always* be sure that the electrical setup is safe, that no circuit is overloaded, and that all power tools and outlets are properly grounded. Do not use power tools in wet locations.

- *Always* read container labels on paints, solvents, and other products; provide ventilation; and observe all other warnings.

- *Always* read the manufacturer's instructions for using a tool, especially the warnings.

- Use hold-downs and push sticks whenever possible when working on a table saw. Avoid working short pieces if you can.

- *Always* remove the key from any drill chuck (portable or press) before starting the drill.

- *Always* pay deliberate attention to how a tool works so that you can avoid being injured.

- *Always* know the limitations of your tools. Do not try to force them to do what they were not designed to do.

- *Always* make sure that any adjustment is locked before proceeding. For example, always check the rip fence on a table saw or the bevel adjustment on a portable saw before starting to work.

- *Always* clamp small pieces to a bench or other work surface when using a power tool.

- *Always* wear the appropriate rubber gloves or work gloves when handling chemicals, moving or stacking lumber, working with concrete, or doing heavy construction.

- *Always* wear a disposable face mask when you create dust by sawing or sanding. Use a special filtering respirator when working with toxic substances and solvents.

- *Always* wear eye protection, especially when using power tools or striking metal on metal or concrete; a chip can fly off, for example, when chiseling concrete.

- *Never* work while wearing loose clothing, hanging hair, open cuffs, or jewelry.

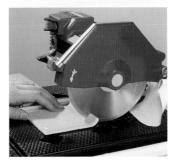

- *Always* be aware that there is seldom enough time for your body's reflexes to save you from injury from a power tool in a dangerous situation; everything happens too fast. Be alert!

- *Always* keep your hands away from the business ends of blades, cutters, and bits.

- *Always* hold a circular saw firmly, usually with both hands.

- *Always* use a drill with an auxiliary handle to control the torque when using large-size bits.

- *Always* check your local building codes when planning new construction. The codes are intended to protect public safety and should be observed to the letter.

- *Never* work with power tools when you are tired or under the influence of alcohol or drugs.

- *Never* cut tiny pieces of wood or pipe using a power saw. When you need a small piece, saw it from a securely clamped longer piece.

- *Never* change a saw blade or a drill or router bit unless the power cord is unplugged. Do not depend on the switch being off. You might accidentally hit it.

- *Never* work in insufficient lighting.

- *Never* work with dull tools. Have them sharpened, or learn how to sharpen them yourself.

- *Never* use a power tool on a workpiece—large or small—that is not firmly supported.

- *Never* saw a workpiece that spans a large distance between horses without close support on each side of the cut; the piece can bend, closing on and jamming the blade, causing saw kickback.

- When sawing, *never* support a workpiece from underneath with your leg or other part of your body.

- *Never* carry sharp or pointed tools, such as utility knives, awls, or chisels, in your pocket. If you want to carry these tools, use a special-purpose tool belt that has leather pockets and holders.

CONTENTS

INTRODUCTION

Ceramic and stone tile have always been used in homes for decoration—and they still are today. Tile is available in an almost endless variety of shapes and colors to suit any house style and any taste. But tile also offers a combination of qualities you won't find in many other building materials. It's extremely durable. It doesn't rot or burn or provide a nesting space or food source for insects. If you install it correctly, tile is one of the few materials that should last as long as your house without a major update or a complete replacement.

Granted, it takes a little longer to install tile than it does to lay down a carpet or slap up a sheet of drywall. But in this book you'll find complete details and step-by-step photos to take you through every type of tile job. You'll get sensible, understandable help with selecting the right materials, using tools safely and effectively, and preparing both existing and new areas for tile jobs that last.

You'll be able to tile kitchens and counters, baths and vanities, floors and walls—using the same techniques as the professionals. And just in case someone drops a heavy pot on your new floor, there's also a complete section on repairs and maintenance.

CHAPTER 1

∎ ∎ ∎

TILE BASICS

Modern ceramic and stone tiles provide hundreds of design options. Unlike many other materials used on floors, walls, and counters, tile does not burn, fade, or easily stain, although some natural stone tiles must be sealed for protection. Tile resists wear better than most interior materials, and they should last as long as the surfaces that support them.

You don't need to pour a concrete slab to support tile, but you do need to beef up floors, countertops, and other surfaces to make them rigid. Even the slight flexing you generate while walking across a wood floor may crack grout seams. But you can easily increase stiffness by adding a layer of plywood or backer board, or by reinforcing the floor frame itself.

The old-fashioned method of installation, called thickset, required careful trowel work to create a thick, level bed of solid mortar that served as a base for the tile. With the modern method, called thinset, there is no need for the mortar bed for most applications. You simply rake out adhesive and start embedding your tiles.

A Short History of Tile

The earliest forms of ceramic tile date back to prehistoric times, when the use of clay as a building material was developed independently in several early cultures. The precursors of modern tile were roughly shaped and not nearly as strong as tiles today. The material was dug from river banks, roughly formed into building blocks, and baked dry in the sun. The first tiles were crude, but even 6,000 years ago people were decorating them by adding pigments for color and carving low-relief designs into their surfaces.

Firing Tile

The ancient Egyptians were the first to discover that firing clay tiles at high temperatures in a kiln made them stronger and more water-resistant. Many ancient cultures also used thin squares of fired clay as decorative elements in their architecture.

Buildings in ancient Mesopotamian cities were fronted with unglazed terra-cotta and colorful decorative tiles. Ancient Greeks and Romans used ceramics for the floors, roofs, and even the plumbing in their buildings. The Chinese used a white clay called kaolin to develop the white-colored and durable ceramic known as porcelain.

Tiles in medieval Europe were generally reserved for the floors of churches. Across the continent, the Byzantines excelled in using tile at a small scale; they created expressive mosaic patterns and murals using ceramic tile as well as pieces of glass and stone.

Glazing Tile

Persian ceramicists, inspired by imported Chinese porcelain, created a decorative tradition that spread across South Asia, North Africa, into Spain with the Moors, and eventually throughout Europe. Because their Islamic religion prohibited using human images in art, artisans turned to brightly colored tiles with ornate and intertwined patterns.

Solid-color glazed tiles were cut and assembled into large-scale mosaics with subtle color gradations. The Islamic artisans also developed metal oxide glazes using tin, copper, cobalt, manganese, and antimony, which made tile glazes more brilliant and durable.

By the fifteenth century, metal oxide-glazed tile had become popular in Italy, and their design influence moved northward with Italian craftsmen. Major European trading centers gave their names to local design motifs and types of tile that are still used, including delft tile (from Delft in Holland), and majolica tile (from Majorca in Spain).

Modern Tile

Today, most commercial tile manufacturers use the pressed-dust method of construction. First, a mixture of ingredients is pressed into the desired tile shape. Then the tile is glazed (or left unglazed) and baked in a kiln. Some tile makers may extrude tile shapes by squeezing them through a press into a die or by rolling them out flat and cutting the tile shapes with a form much like a cookie cutter.

Whatever the method, all ceramic tile must be fired to become durable. The purity of the clay, the number of firings, and the temperature of the kiln determine the quality and price. Kiln temperatures vary from about 900° F to 2,500° F. Lower firing temperatures produce more porous tile and soft glazes; higher temperatures produce dense, nonporous tile and hard glazes.

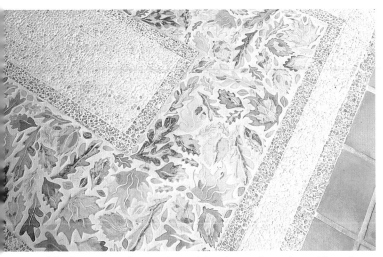

Modern mosaics *and combinations of stock and hand-made tiles can be just as intricate as ancient patterns.*

Ancient artisans *created intricate shapes with small tiles, such as this pattern in a church at Mount Nebo in Jordan.*

Decorative tiles *were used in complex color and pattern combinations, as on this ancient building in Jerusalem.*

Tile Characteristics

There are several types of ceramic tile and many ways to categorize them. The built-in properties can make one better than another for a particular installation.

Firing & Glazes

When most tile is first formed it has to dry enough to become stable. Then it goes into a kiln at temperatures ranging from about 2,000° F to 2,500° F. Tiles fired at lower temperatures generally are more porous and have softer glazes than tiles fired at higher temperatures.

These surface coatings can be used to add color and decoration, and to protect the tile body. Color is commonly included in a mixture of pigments that is added before the tile is fired or applied to a hardened tile and bonded with a second firing. Glazed tiles range from a high-gloss to a dull matte finish.

Water Absorption

There are four basic categories of tile rated by how much water they absorb. More porous tiles are generally softer and absorb more water. They are less expensive, however. Less-porous tiles generally are harder and may be more expensive.

Nonvitreous tile absorbs about 7% or more water; semivitreous tile absorbs between 3% and 7% water; vitreous tile absorbs between 0.6% and 3% water, and impervious tile absorbs 0.5% or less water. Generally, the longer the firing time and the higher the firing temperature, the more nonporous (or vitreous) the tile. Vitreous and impervious tiles include ceramic and glass mosaic varieties, as well as porcelain tiles. Don't use nonvitreous or semivitreous tiles outdoors in cold climates. Water trapped in the tile body will alternately freeze and thaw, cracking the tile.

Tile porosity becomes important in the choice of tiles for wet conditions such as a tub surround because water absorbed by porous tiles can harbor bacteria and eventually penetrate the substrate, loosening the tile bond.

Tile Selection

When you visit your tile dealer, the ceramic tile probably will be divided into basic categories of wall, floor, and ceramic mosaic tile. There are also many specialty tiles. (See pages 18 to 33 for more on tile materials.)

Modern ceramic tile *allows you to cover different surfaces with a multihued tile that ties a room together.*

Floor Tiles. Most glazed floor tiles work on counter-tops and other horizontal surfaces subject to heavy use. Some may be too heavy to set on walls without special supports during the installation, such as a batten board or a row of nails. Some come in sizes up to 24 inches square and may be unwieldy and out of scale as wall tile. Glazed floor tiles often are listed in manufacturers' cata-logs as glazed quarry tile or glazed pavers. Generally, you use glazed floor tiles on interior floors only. But some glazed floor tiles have a fine carbide grit incorporated into the glaze to make them slip-resistant in wet areas.

Wall Tiles. Wall tiles generally are thin, lightweight, nonvitreous (porous) tiles coated with a soft glaze. Most don't have the strength to stand up to floor traf-fic. You also can use sheet tile mounted on a backing of paper, plastic mesh, or fabric mesh. The sheets elimi-nate the laborious process of spacing individual tiles but are usually more expensive.

Ceramic Mosaic Tiles. All tiles that are 2 inches square or smaller are considered mosaic tiles. Generally, these dense-bodied vitreous tiles resist water, stains, impact, frost, and abrasion, making them suitable for practically any application. Shapes include squares, rec-tangles, hexagons, circles, teardrops, clover leafs, and random pebble designs, among others. Most ceramic mosaic tiles are mounted on a backing sheet.

Antique Tiles. Although some rare old tiles command very high prices, others are relatively affordable. All are collectible, including Victorian art tiles, Arts and Crafts tiles, and Art Deco tiles, among others. If you can't find the real thing, check with companies specializing in imported hand-painted tiles. Many include a selection of reproduction antique designs.

Hand-Painted and Mural Tiles. Large tile manufac-turers offer a broad selection of domestic and imported hand-painted tiles. Several even employ a staff of artists to make personalized hand-painted tiles to order, as do small independent artisans and ceramic shops. Hand-painted tiles are available as individual accents to spruce up a kitchen countertop or fireplace surround. Some hand-painted tiles have sculptured surfaces, while others are hand-cut into unusual shapes. Custom-made hand-painted tiles vary widely in price—from $20 to $100 per piece—depending on whether they are chosen from stock designs or are custom-made to your specifications. If hand-painted tiles are too costly, most tile dealers also carry decorator tiles and picture tiles with silk screen or decal designs at a more affordable price.

Ceramic tiles with interlocking patterns can form a centerpiece by themselves or in a surrounding field of tile.

While ancient mosaics were installed piece by piece (left); intricate patterns are available on full tiles (right).

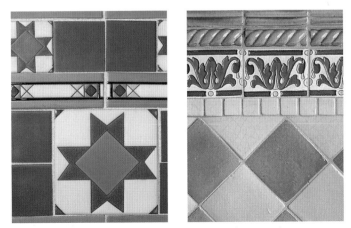

Larger tiles, trim strips, and accent tiles can be com-bined into highly decorative and colorful panels.

Tile Sizes & Shapes

Field tiles come in several different shapes, which you can use singly or in various combinations to form patterns. The actual size of these tiles may vary ⅛ inch more or less, as will the thickness, depending on the manufacturer. This means you can't always mix tiles from different manufacturers.

Single Tiles

This is the type of ceramic tile that most do-it-yourselfers use: single tiles laid one at a time. They are available in a great variety of sizes, colors, and patterns. Most custom decorative and hand-painted tiles fall into this category as well. Tiles typically are ¼ to ⅜ inch thick and range in size from 1 × 1 inch to 12 × 12 inches square, although larger sizes and different shapes are available. Most often, layouts work out with a grid of field tiles and at least some partial tiles around the edges. The size you find listed in a manufacturer's catalog generally is nominal and not actual. It generally includes an allowance for grout.

Sheet-Mounted Tiles

Sheet tiles are evenly spaced tiles mounted on a backing sheet of paper, plastic mesh, or fabric mesh. They may also may be joined by small dabs of vinyl, polyurethane, or silicone rubber in a process called dot-mounting. Many sheets are 12 inches square or larger. It's wise to use sheet-mounted applications on small tiles that would be very time-consuming to set one by one. Small sizes on sheets provide the option of laying tiles on gentle curves. All sheet-mounted tiles require grouting once installed.

Pregrouted Tile Panels

Eliminating the need to grout joints sounds like a good idea. And some tile outlets may offer pregrouted tile panels to do the job. But the grout is actually a flexible polyurethane, polyvinyl chloride, rubber grout, or silicone caulk. Without rigid grout between tiles, these sheets often are flexible enough to bend and stretch with normal building movement. A variety of trim pieces generally are available to complete the installation. You use tubes of matching silicone caulk to grout the joints between panel edges and trim pieces. Typically, the grout is treated with a special mildew and fungus inhibitor, making these panels suitable for shower and tub enclosures. Because of this chemical treatment, the Food and Drug Administration does not recommend installing the sheets on kitchen countertops or on other serving and food-preparation areas. These flexible grouts typically are available in white and a wide range of colors.

Basic Sizes & Shapes

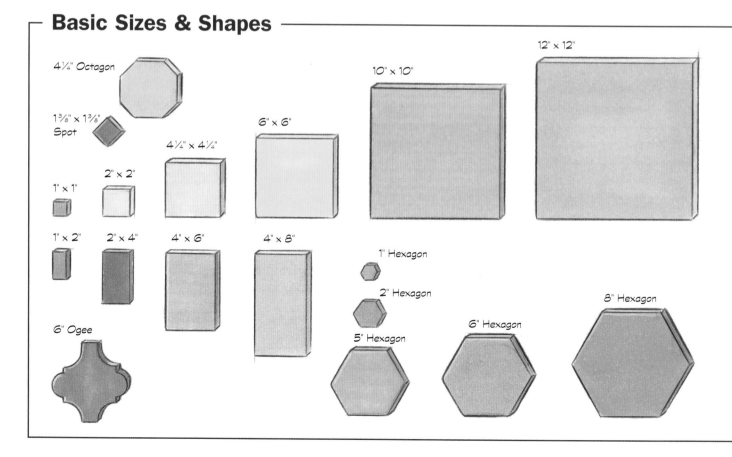

4¼" Octagon

1⅜" × 1⅜" Spot

1" × 1"

2" × 2"

4¼" × 4¼"

6" × 6"

10" × 10"

12" × 12"

1" × 2"

2" × 4"

4" × 6"

4" × 8"

6" Ogee

1" Hexagon

2" Hexagon

5" Hexagon

6" Hexagon

8" Hexagon

Trim & Specialty Tile

All tiles that are not field tiles are referred to as trim tiles. They are used to create smooth, finished edges and corners for specific areas. In tile catalogs, manufacturers usually picture the available sizes and shapes of trim pieces for different tiles in their line.

◆ *Angles.* These tiles include inside and outside corners that create sharp turns instead of rounded edges.

◆ *Aprons.* Half-size tiles called aprons are used to fill in narrow areas, such as along the front of a countertop.

◆ *Bases.* Tiles designed specifically for the floor line, called base trims or runners, have a finished top edge. They are used in areas where the floor has been tiled but the wall has not.

◆ *Beads.* These trims are sometimes called quarter-rounds, and are used to finish off corners and edges. The narrow pieces turn a rounded, 90-degree angle.

◆ *Bullnose.* These are regular field tiles with one curved and finished edge. They neatly trim a course of tile that ends without turning a corner. Often, a bullnose tile is paired with an apron tile meeting the bullnose at a right angle. The result is a smoothly turned corner and edge. There are surface bullnose tiles designed for thin-set installations and radiused bullnose designed for thicker, mortar-bed installations.

◆ *Countertop Trims.* These trim pieces are set on the outside edge of a countertop. The raised lip is designed to prevent drips. Many V-cap tiles have this feature.

◆ *Coves.* These pieces are used to gently turn corners at a right angle. The corner can turn either inward or outward. Cove base turns a corner at floor level. Special cove pieces that have a finished edge turn a corner at the top row of a backsplash. Other cove pieces do not have finished edges.

◆ *Miters.* Two miter pieces together form a corner separated by a grout joint.

◆ *Rounds.* These trim tiles create a rounded corner instead of an angular one.

◆ *Swimming-Pool Edging.* These tiles are designed to cover the coping on swimming pools. They require a thickset mortar bed.

◆ *V-caps.* Although they are called V-shaped, these edging tiles often are more L-shaped to cover the perimeter of a counter, for example, and wrap around the front edge of plywood and backer board.

◆ *Windowsill Trim.* Windowsill tile has a finished edge on one side and a rounded corner on the other. It covers the sill itself and turns to meet the tile on the wall. Without this trim piece, you would need two tiles: a flat field tile for the sill itself and a quarter-round to turn the corner. Sill trim simplifies the installation.

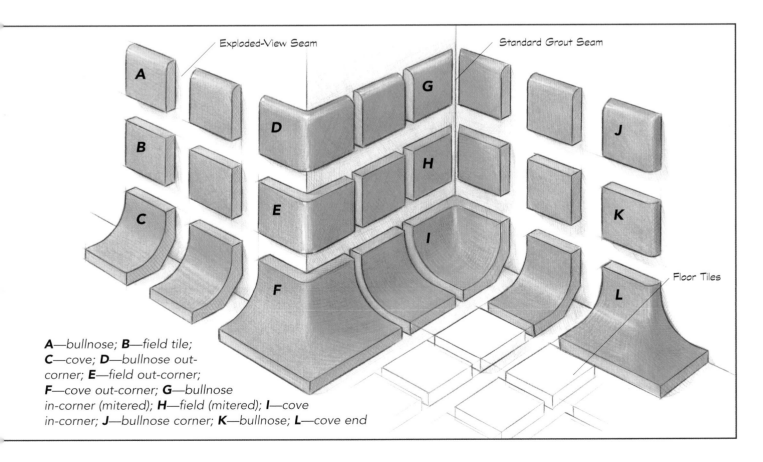

A—bullnose; *B*—field tile; *C*—cove; *D*—bullnose out-corner; *E*—field out-corner; *F*—cove out-corner; *G*—bullnose in-corner (mitered); *H*—field (mitered); *I*—cove in-corner; *J*—bullnose corner; *K*—bullnose; *L*—cove end

••• CERAMIC TILE •••

Ceramic tile isn't very complicated. Most pieces are nothing more than some clay flattened into a square shape, covered with a hard glaze, and baked in a very high temperature oven. Pretty simple. It's also been around for a while—from what we can tell, about 6,000 years. As such, it's a clear-cut example of established technology. Not much need for a computer chip in these things, at least not right now.

The term might be as clear as a prophet and as old as the hills, but unfortunately, it's a little general. So many different tiles, used in so many different places, are all called ceramic that buying tile can be a bit confusing. Probably the best way out of the fog is to think of ceramic tile as the default product among many other specialized offerings. It's the stuff on your bathroom walls, your brother-in-law's vanity top, and around the top edge of your neighbor's swimming pool.

Ceramic tile comes in a variety of different sizes, colors, and surface finishes. These days, it's usually installed over a cementitious backer board and embedded in a layer of thinset mortar. Tile is rated by its water resistance. A rating by PEI (Porcelain Enamel Institute) of 1 or 2 means that the tile can be used only on walls. A rating of 3 or 4 makes a tile suitable for all residential applications: floors, walls, and countertops.

The difference between the ratings is primarily the result of how the tile is made. A low temperature (1,200° F) firing in the kiln will create a more porous tile, which would be bad for a floor where exposure to moisture is high. When a tile is fired at a higher temperature (over 2,000° F) the result is a denser tile with a harder surface that can be used in any residential application anywhere.

Walls and Borders

Ceramic Shower Surround

Patterned Backsplash

Two-Tone Color Scheme

Ceramic Accents

▪▪▪ PORCELAIN TILE ▪▪▪

Although porcelain tile can sometimes look like common ceramic tile, there are some big differences. First off, porcelain units are made of carefully refined white clay that is fired at an extremely high temperature. As a result, the individual tiles are very dense and much less porous than ceramic tile, which makes them more water resistant. Porcelain tile is also much harder than ceramic tile, so it wears better and longer and is almost impossible to stain. This makes porcelain a good choice for floors and countertops inside the house and for exterior applications where the freeze-and-thaw cycle is an issue.

Another difference: most porcelain tiles are not glazed. The color of the tile is achieved by colored dyes that are added to the clay during manufacture. Because of this, the same color goes throughout the entire tile, instead of being only in the glaze. So if the floor is scratched, the damage is less noticeable. The lack of glaze also allows some subtlety in surface texture. Finer, more intricate patterns can be pressed into the tile. If glaze were added to these tiles, this texture would be lost. The lack of glaze also allows porcelain tile to look more like natural stone tile. With the addition of appropriate color and surface details, porcelain can mimic granite, marble, slate, and other stone products. They look like stone but perform better because the porcelain isn't as brittle.

In most cases, porcelain tiles are installed like ceramic tiles. This means over a cementitious backer board and in thinset mortar. The mortar should, however, be latex reinforced. Because the porcelain tiles are so dense, they don't absorb much mortar, so the stronger bond achieved by latex additives is required.

Porcelain Floor Tiles

Stone Look-Alike

Geometric Pattern

Terra-Cotta Color Backsplash

Stone Backsplash

▪▪▪ STONE TILE ▪▪▪

Many types of natural stone tiles are available for residential use, both for the inside and outside of the house. The most popular are probably granite, marble, and slate. Of the three, granite is the hardest and densest. It usually comes with a polished surface that makes it water- and stain-resistant. Marble is softer than granite and slate is softer than marble. Both need to be sealed to prevent staining and water damage.

Stone tile tends to cost more per square foot (often $5 to $10) compared to ceramic tile (in the neighborhood of $2 to $3 per foot). But stone tiles have such a distinctive appearance that many people find them irresistible. The variable colors and patterns that are found in natural stone can't be reproduced anywhere else, and no two tiles are exactly alike.

For interior use, granite and marble are usually sold with both surfaces cut smooth and at a consistent thickness. Slate is often sold with one side split and the other side (that will face down into the mortar) cut flat. This yields a somewhat rough floor surface with good traction that many people prefer for kitchens, foyers, and mudrooms. The most popular size is a 12 × 12 inches. But many others sizes are available for creating patterns. Often these less common sizes are not stock items and need to be ordered.

Stone tiles require an underlayment of cementitious backer board and are usually set in latex reinforced thinset mortar. Most people seem to prefer very thin grout joints for granite and marble, and a wider grout joint (up to about ⅜ in.) for slate. One of the drawbacks of using stone tiles is the limited selection of trim pieces. This isn't usually a problem on floors, but it can be more frustrating on walls and countertops.

Slate Entry

Tumbled Marble Walls

Stone Insets

Granite Walls

Marble Tub Surround

▪▪▪ GLASS TILE ▪▪▪

Glass tiles, as the name indicates, are made of pieces of glass formed into standard tile sizes. Countless colors and many different textures are available, from smooth to rough. At the extremes, these tiles can be almost transparent and nearly opaque. For the most part, glass tiles are used as accent tiles, almost always on walls. Perhaps the most popular location is on a kitchen countertop backsplash. Glass may be impervious to stains and water damage, but it is prone to cracking and scratching. So it's generally considered inappropriate for floor use.

Glass tiles have a completely different appearance than typical ceramic tiles because light moves through all but the most opaque pieces. This makes the tiles seem to vibrate slightly, which catches the eye. Add to this the fact that many of the available color options are very vibrant, and you get something that doesn't fade into the background. Glass tiles look more like stained glass, Tiffany lamps, and fruit-flavored hard candy than they do the standard white ceramic tile.

This product is pretty expensive. Prices of $15 per square foot are not uncommon. When this is compared with ceramic tile that costs $2 to $3 a square foot, it's easy to see why glass tiles are often used as accents. These tiles are also commonly available in mosaic sheets of 1 × 1-inch tiles.

As with most other tiles, glass units should be installed over cementitious backer board. But instead of standard thinset mortar, choose a white latex reinforced thinset mortar. Because you can see through most glass tiles, the white background changes the color of the tile less than a dark-gray mortar would. Standard grout is recommended for glass tile. But because the glass is so impervious to any moisture, it takes longer to set than it would with ceramic tile.

Sparkling Backsplash

Bright-Red Accents

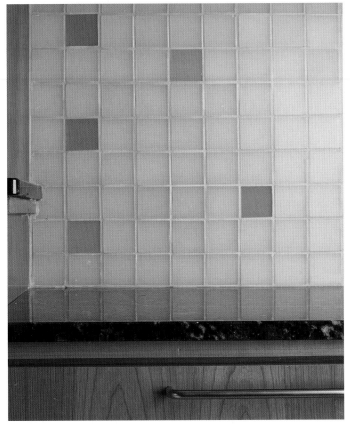

Transparent Design

Shimmering Wall Treatment

▪▪▪ TERRA-COTTA TILE ▪▪▪

Terra-cotta, which means "cooked earth" in Italian, is one of the oldest and most popular tiles in the world. And in many places, it has been made the same way for centuries. Unlike typical ceramic tiles, traditional terra-cotta tiles are not glazed. They are made of unrefined clay baked at comparatively low temperature. Their color is dependent on where the clay comes from. Large producers of terra-cotta like Italy, Portugal, and Mexico have different colors. But tiles from the same country and the same batch can still have a good deal of variation in their hue. This lack of uniformity is considered an attribute, not a failing, to terra-cotta buyers.

Because most terra-cotta tiles lack glaze and are very porous, they soak up water easily. So they need to be sealed thoroughly after they're installed, and resealed periodically to keep them looking their best. Otherwise, staining is inevitable. This natural porosity also prevents terra-cotta from being installed outside if it will be exposed to freezing temperatures.

Terra-cotta tiles come in a wide range of shapes and sizes. Some are nearly as uniform in dimension as ceramic tile. But many terra-cotta products are hand made and therefore vary in size and thickness quite a bit. For interior applications, terra-cotta should be applied over a cementitious backer board and in a bed of latex reinforced thinset mortar. In recent years, glazed terra-cotta tiles have become much more popular. A wide range of brilliant color alternatives is available, as are tiles with hand-painted drawings and engravings.

Rustic Elegance

Cooking-Center Application

Traditional Coloring

Contemporary Coloring

Diagonal Pattern

■■■ DECORATIVE TILE BORDERS ■■■

Although ceramic tile is a wonderful surface finish that is considered by most people to be an upscale design choice, a whole wall or floor of one kind of tile can seem a little monolithic, a little bit like too much of a good thing. This is where decorative borders come to the rescue. These borders can be as simple as a contrasting color of the same tile installed around the perimeter of a kitchen floor. Or they can be more elaborate, like an entirely different type, size, shape, and color of tile used as a kind of chair rail on a bathroom wall.

Border tiles are often high gloss, brightly colored, and heavily textured. Tile stores may have lots of different choices when it comes to field tiles (the ones you use for most of a floor or wall) but will have many fewer decorative tiles. Decorative units can be expensive and a whole wall or floor of these tiles can be visually overwhelming.

Fortunately, the Internet is loaded with different tile design studios that may have decorative tiles that you like. One of the most distinctive types of wall borders is called listello tile. These tiles are usually thicker than the field tiles, so they will stand proud of the wall. They also have molded or embossed patterns, and the most expensive versions are hand painted.

If you plan to integrate a decorative border into a field of standard ceramic tiles, make sure the sizes of the tiles are compatible. Take one of your field tiles along when shopping for decorative units. No matter what you chose, the installation requirements for the decorative tiles will be the same as for the field tiles you are putting on the wall or floor.

Seashell Theme

Playful Accents

Border Styles

Adding Texture

Bright Frames

••• PAINTED TILE •••

Painted tile is really a subset of all tiles. If you want to go through the trouble, any tile can be painted and then glazed or sealed. The only real question is how expensive it will be. It's not unheard of for an individual 4 × 4-inch painted tile to cost nearly $100. But a much more common price is between $10 and $30. That's a lot of money, but if used judiciously, painted tiles can have a tremendous impact on a room without breaking the budget.

One of the most effective uses of these tiles is in a wall mural. These are often designed for the backsplash area above the kitchen countertop or the inside of a tiled shower stall. For centuries, mosaic tiles have been painted to create striking landscapes, portraits, and still lifes that were incorporated into the overall design of floors, walls, and even ceilings.

Some painted tiles are called art tiles. This term generally refers to hand-made units that are used as accents in other tile installations. As you might expect, these tiles are available in a wide range of colors, sizes, and designs—in fact, there are as many types as there are artisans creating them. Depending on how these tiles are made, they may not be as durable as typical manufactured tiles. Make sure the ones you select will perform well where you plan to use them. If this can't be determined, use these tiles only in areas that don't get much wear or exposure to moisture.

You can create painted accent tiles yourself if you are lucky enough to have a ceramic crafts store nearby. Some of these places will let you paint blank tiles, and then they'll coat them with a clear glaze and fire them so that they will perform like a manufactured tile.

Cooking-Center Theme

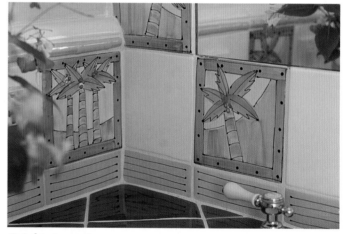

Bright Accents

Fireplace Accents

Mood Setters

··· MOSAIC TILE ···

One way to gauge progress over the years is to look at mosaic tile. For centuries, these small tiles (usually ¾- to 2-inch squares) were set individually no matter what the size of the job. A cathedral was treated pretty much the same way as the entry area to a typical home. But finally someone came up with the idea of joining these tiles together in 12-inch-square mats with the tiles glued to a mesh. If you were using 1-inch tiles on a job, laying down one of these sheets made things go about 144 times faster. Not bad, no matter how you define progress.

Today mosaic tiles come in different sizes, shapes, colors, and materials—though glazed ceramic tile and porcelain tile are the most popular. They are commonly used on floors and walls and are installed over cementitious backer board in a bed of thinset mortar. The small size, however, makes them very popular for other striking treatments, including decorative borders, murals, and one-of-a-kind custom renderings for the luxury residential market. You can also get individual mosaic tiles, instead of sheets, if you just want to accent a plain field of single-color tile.

The small size of mosaic tile is not only distinctive, it also makes for easier installation, especially around pipes and other obstructions. All you have to do to remove a tile is cut it from the mesh backing with a utility knife. In fact, mosaic tiles are the product of choice if you're tiling curved or rounded surfaces. Another plus for mosaic floor tiles is the great traction they yield because they have so many grout joints per square foot of floor space.

Themed Backsplash

Colorful Design

Mosaic Border

Traditional Design

Custom Application

Room Prep: Structure

Stripping Drywall

By using partial tiles and adjusting the layout of field tiles, you can compensate for minor irregularities on walls. But sometimes you need to do more than prepare an old surface with joint compound and work on the framing underneath. When you need to strip away drywall, take a cautious approach to avoid cutting or damaging pipes and wires that could be in the wall. If there are outlets, radiators, or hot-air registers close by, you should peel the surface instead of trying more vigorous demolition.

Finding Seams. If the drywall is so well taped that you can't spot the seams, use a stud finder to locate the vertical strip of nails over studs. The stud with two rows is under the seam between panels.

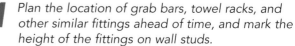

1 The first step is to pull any trim on top of the panel you need to remove. Pry baseboards and other pieces with a flat bar placed over studs.

Removing a Wall Stud

When you find one or two studs that are throwing the wall out of kilter or studs damaged by rot, replace them. Because wall studs are nailed through horizontal pieces at the top and bottom of the wall, you can't get at these nails to pull them. The most practical plan is to cut the stud you want to remove in half and pry out the pieces one at a time. If you are replacing several studs in a load-bearing wall, the safest approach is to install one or two temporary braces until the new studs are in place.

Trimming Nails. Where sharp nails remain in the top and bottom frame of the wall, slice them off flush with a hacksaw or reciprocating saw fitted with a metal-cutting blade.

1 Use a reciprocating saw or a saber saw to start cutting through the damaged stud about halfway up the wall. Stay clear of pipes or wires.

Adding Studs & Braces

To beef up a weak stud, or double up framing to provide additional support for new drywall, you can add a stud with construction adhesive and screws. This generally makes a more secure connection than nails alone, and it is less likely to disrupt the finish on nearby wall surfaces. If you have the wall frame exposed, it's also wise to install braces, such as 2x4s on the flat, wherever you will attach fittings through tile, such as towel racks or grab bars.

Recording Brace Locations. Before covering a wall brace with new drywall, measure and record its exact distance from the floor. This beats drilling holes through your new tile that turn out to be in the wrong places.

1 Plan the location of grab bars, towel racks, and other similar fittings ahead of time, and mark the height of the fittings on wall studs.

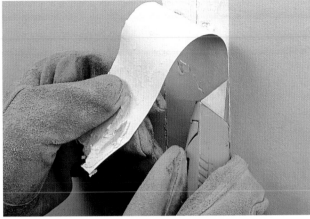

2 Once you locate the seam, use a utility knife to cut through the coats of compound. Peel away the paper tape to expose nailed edges of the panels.

3 After you pull some of the nails, pry on the panel, which will crack in large sections. Then pull the remaining nails in the studs.

2 To keep the stud from binding on the saw blade (even if you cut by hand) insert a wedge to keep the cut open as you complete the job.

3 Once you cut through, pry out the stud in two pieces. Remember to trim the nails driven through the top and bottom of the wall frame.

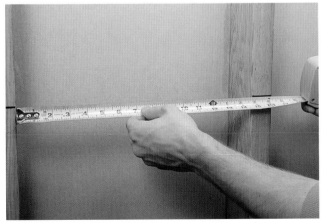

2 Measure the space between studs, and cut a brace to fit between them. If you're not sure about the exact height, use a wide board.

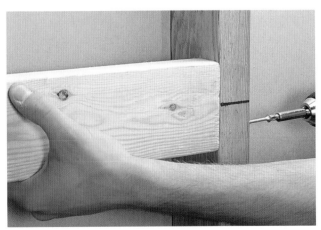

3 A solid 2x4 set flush with the framing and screwed through adjacent studs provides a solid backup for surface-mounted hardware.

Room Prep: Baths

Removing a Sink

Although you can tile up to or over a sink edge, in most cases you need to remove the unit before tiling the counter. Most sinks will release after you unscrew the small fittings below the counter that keep it in place. You also may have to slice through a layer of caulk under the sink lip. The job can get a bit more complicated when you need to disconnect the water supply and drainpipes. The first step, of course, is to cut off the water supply. Then you can go to work on the sink drain, the fixture mountings, and the trap.

Balky Joints. Although many new drain fittings have a wide flange and are designed to be turned only hand-tight, you may need a Stilson wrench to release old connections.

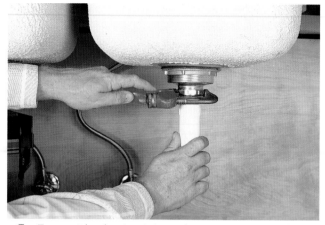

1 Even with plastic piping, the connection to the drain tailpiece is usually metal. You need to loosen it with a wrench.

Removing a Toilet

It's not a pleasant job, to be sure. But if you skip the sometimes difficult process of removing the toilet, you may find that tiling up to the base causes problems. First, you'll have to trim tiles around the edges, some of which are curved. Second, the grout seam may not last because the connection is subject to stress. Instead, remove the unit so that you can extend tile under the base.

A New Wax Seal. You'll find that the hidden connection between the toilet and the drain is sealed with a wax ring. Don't try to reuse the existing ring. Scrape away the old material around the drain and install a new one before setting the fixture back in place.

1 Start by turning off the water at the cutoff valve. Then loosen the holding nut, and release the supply pipe. You can leave it attached to the fixture.

Sanitary Sills

There are many ways to make a transition between slightly different floor levels—for example, where new plywood or backer board and tile raises the floor in a bath. Some sills cover the tile edge, so you install them after the job. In baths, it's customary to install a piece of marble, called a sanitary sill. Because it often starts off the main field and controls the layout, you should install this sill before tiling. It's also wise to try a dry run, setting down samples of underlayment and tile, to see how the different levels and different materials will join the sill.

Setting Marble. Use pressure or a rubber mallet to set the sill. Marble is brittle and can crack easily under excessive force or sharp blows.

1 You may need to strip back flooring, such as ¾-in. oak, to install a marble sill. To prevent cracking, the subfloor should be flat and smooth.

2 Use a long-handled basin wrench to reach behind a sink and unscrew fittings that connect the water lines to the faucet fixture.

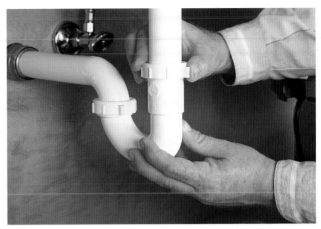

3 If you have trouble disconnecting the tailpiece, try loosening the drain line at the trap. Plug the hole temporarily to stop sewer gas from escaping.

2 After you drain the holding tank and bowl, remove the cover caps along the base rim, and unscrew the nuts holding the fixture to the drain.

3 Scrape away old wax around the drain flange. You may want to temporarily stuff up the drain to keep sewer gas from escaping.

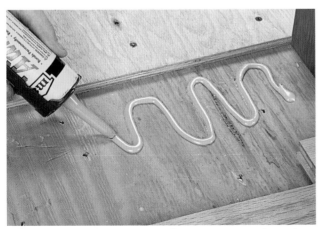

2 Spread a liberal bead of adhesive over the sub-floor. If you use a synthetic sill, check the manufacturer's recommendation for adhesive.

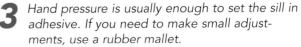

3 Hand pressure is usually enough to set the sill in adhesive. If you need to make small adjustments, use a rubber mallet.

Room Prep: Kitchens

Installing Lights & Switches

In any room where you plan to tile, it pays to install wiring ahead of time as part of the room preparation. Fishing cable through framing and cutting into walls is too likely to disrupt tile and grout seams if you do this work later on. Also, you can plan ahead so that outlets and switches fall evenly in the tile grid. Or you may be able to locate a kitchen switch box, for example, in a strip of existing drywall above the tiled backsplash.

Safety. Remember to cut electrical power to the circuit you are working on, and test exposed wire leads to be doubly sure the power is off. If in doubt about electrical codes and practices, leave this work to a licensed electrician.

1 *Often you can take power for a kitchen light from a nearby fixture box. In this case, it's in the floor framing just below the kitchen.*

Removing Old Vinyl

Many kitchens have a utilitarian floor made of vinyl that's considerably less expensive than tile. When you upgrade, it's wise to peel away the old material. (If you use a heat gun, bear in mind that some reach very high temperatures.) Resilient flooring generally does not provide the kind of rigid support that tile and grout requires. Also, the sheet flooring may have been installed to cover up problems that you need to fix before tiling.

Adhesive on Drywall. Take the extra time to reheat and scrape away old adhesive left after you remove the base. If you take the base along with chunks of drywall, you'll have to do a lot of repair work to provide a flat surface for the new tile.

1 *To minimize repair work on the drywall surface, use a heat gun (or a hair dryer in a pinch) to loosen the vinyl adhesive.*

Tiling to Wood Trim

If you are working in existing spaces, you may be able to remove just the quarter-round or other trim strips along baseboards, and reinstall them after tiling. Casings around doors are more difficult to deal with because they generally protrude more into the room. There are two basic options. One is to slice off just enough of the bottom of the casing to allow your tile to slip in underneath. The other is to butt the tile to the casing, and cut it to match the contour of the trim. This can be very time consuming on complex molding.

Planning Thickness. Start the cut with several backward strokes. Then cut back and forth, keeping the blade flat on the stack of materials.

1 *To make room for new tile under existing trim, use a piece of underlayment and a full tile as a depth guide for your saw.*

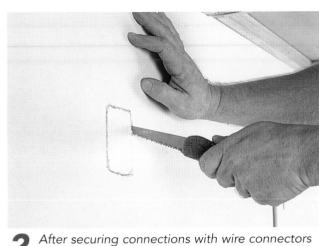

2 After securing connections with wire connectors and closing the box, mark and cut the opening for the light switch under the cabinets.

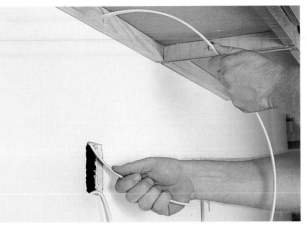

3 You can fish the power leg up through the wall framing and the switch leg down from an opening in the back of the cabinets.

2 As the adhesive bond loosens, use a drywall knife to pry the base away from the wall. You may need to work on one small section at a time.

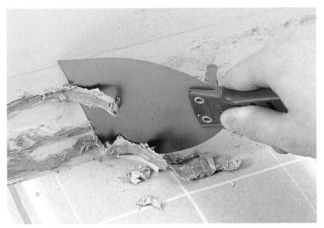

3 Reheat the remaining adhesive, if necessary, and scrape away any raised ribs. Thin deposits will be covered over with tile adhesive.

2 To butt tile against existing trim, copy the outline with a contour gauge. Small pins match the outline when you press it against the molding.

3 Another option is to mark the butt tile with a compass, scribing the cut. To be accurate, keep the pin end and the pencil end parallel as you mark.

Patterns & Working Lines

There are many ways to set tiles. For example, you can start with full-size tiles at the most visible part of a room, such as the doorway, and leave partial tiles or irregular cuts for an out-of-the-way wall. Most often, the best layout approach is to center the main field of full tiles in the area, and adjust the field to leave partial tiles that are about the same size around the edges. But within this general framework, you have many options.

Basic Tile Patterns

Whether you combine different sizes of tile or stick to a basic grid, there are several basic patterns.

Jack-on-Jack. This is the most straightforward way to install tile: in a grid with tiles stacked one on top of the other. The grout seams line up vertically and horizontally. Trimming is easy because the tiles are square or rectangular like the shapes of floors and walls.

Diagonal Jack-on-Jack. This pattern is basic jack-on-jack rotated 45 degrees. The grout lines run on a diagonal. The diamond effect of this pattern has a drawback, though. Wherever the corners of tiles meet a floor or wall, you have to trim off the point to create a horizontal or vertical edge. This system often looks best in a frame of square tiles.

Running Bond. This system adjusts the basic jack-on-jack by setting the center of full tiles over the grout seam in the course below. The offset creates a less defined edge than a squared-up grid, which can help to deemphasize irregular border cuts.

Establishing Working Lines

Once the pattern is established, the tile is selected, and the surface is prepared, you need to plan out working lines that will help you position the tiles. Generally you make these lines by snapping the chalk-laden string from a chalk-line box. Instead of snapping two lines close together, one line is centered in the grout joint.

Lines for a Square-Cornered Room. If the room is relatively square, the standard approach is to snap wall-to-wall chalk lines that cross in the center. Starting at the intersection, either dry-lay a row of tiles along each working line, or use a layout stick to determine where cut tiles are needed and what size they will be. Be sure to include the width of grout joints. If a row of partial tiles along one wall is less than half a tile wide, reposition the tiles so that the cut row is half a tile or wider. If the layout results in a narrow row of cut tiles, make the grout joints a bit wider to eliminate that row. If the last tile against the wall is almost the width of a full tile, make all the grout joints a bit narrower. That way you can fit a full row of tiles in the space.

Working-Line Options

Square-Cornered Room

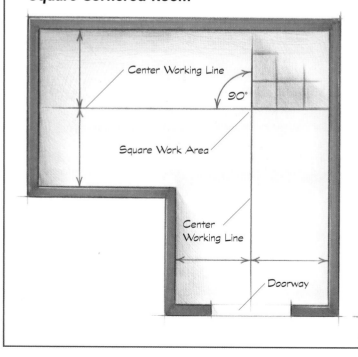

Center Working Line
90°
Square Work Area
Center Working Line
Doorway

Out-of-Square Room

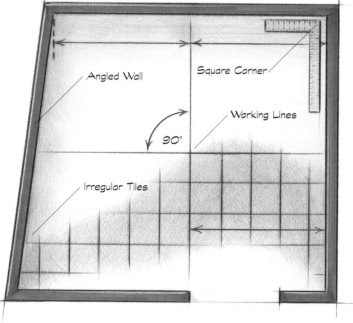

Angled Wall
Square Corner
Working Lines
90°
Irregular Tiles

Lines for an Out-of-Square Room. If the room is out-of-square, one approach is to align tile with the most prominent wall, and make irregular cuts as needed against the other walls. To determine which corner is most square, place a tile tightly against the walls in each corner of the room. Project chalk lines from the outside corner of each tile in both directions. Then check the intersections of the chalk lines at each corner for square, and choose the one that is closest to 90 degrees. Then try a dry layout. You may need to lay out a row of tiles or use a layout stick in several locations because cut tiles may work on one end of a wall but not the other.

Lines for an L-Shaped Room. Divide the room into two sections, and snap layout lines. Adjust the lines so that all intersections are at 90 degrees. Adjust lines as necessary so that cut tiles around the room's perimeter will be larger than half a tile.

Lines for an Adjoining Room. When you extend the tile field into an adjoining room, be sure to line up the grout lines. If the doorway or pass-through is wide, try to center the tiles so that cut tiles on each side are of the same width. But check to see how this arrangement effects the overall layout where tiles meet the walls.

If you are using large tiles, it helps to use additional working lines to ensure that the grout joints align properly and are of approximately the same width. Typically, you add these extra lines in a grid. Each square in the grid can contain four, six, or nine tiles with the lines representing the middle of the grout joints between the tiles. Fill in one block at a time, adjusting the tiles so that all of the grout joints are evenly spaced.

Lines for a Diagonal Layout. When you lay tiles diagonally, you need a second set of working lines. From the intersection of the original working lines, measure out an equal distance along any three of the lines, and drive a nail at these points. Hook the end of a measuring tape to one of the nails, and hold a pencil against the tape at a distance equal to that between the nails and center point. Use the tape and pencil as a compass to scribe two sets of arcs on the floor. This will provide points along the 45-degree diagonal.

Your diagonal lines will line up with grout joints between tiles. Ideally, the original lines that are square in the room should slice through the corners of the tiles. You may need to adjust the working lines to achieve the best pattern of partial tiles at all four walls. (This is where the dry layout comes into play again.) When setting the tiles, fill in one quadrant at a time.

You may also need additional working lines if you are laying unusually shaped tiles. With an interlocking shape such as an ogee that does not have fully square sides, you can snap lines as a guide for the end points or other prominent edges of the tile.

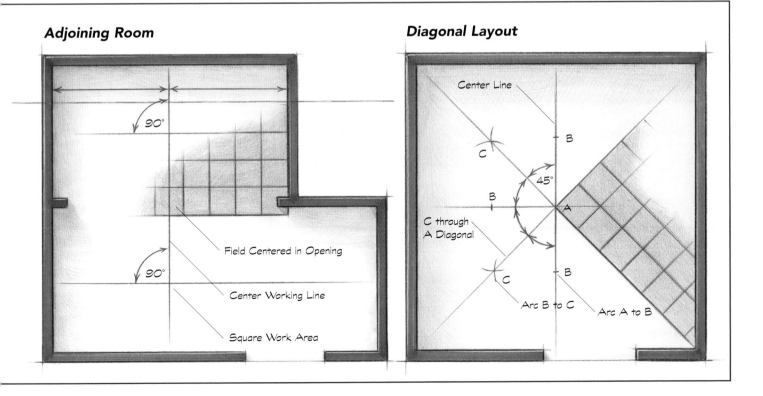

Adjoining Room

90°
90°
Field Centered in Opening
Center Working Line
Square Work Area

Diagonal Layout

Center Line
B
C
45°
B
A
C through A Diagonal
C
B
Arc B to C
Arc A to B

CHAPTER 2

■■■

TOOLS & MATERIALS

If you are an active do-it-yourselfer, you probably own most of the tools you'll need for tile work. You may want to buy a few specialized tile tools, such as a wet saw, but you can also rent them. If you are in the process of accumulating how-to tools, consider these general buying guidelines. They can help you collect practical products for all kinds of repair and improvement projects.

Durability. Buy better quality in tools you'll use often, such as a hammer and saw. Don't pay for heavy-duty contractor tools you'll use occasionally.

Precision. Buy tools that are in the ballpark of your skill level, with features you can really use. Stick with basic tools designed to do one job well. Avoid multipurpose gimmick tools.

Strength. Look for hammers, wrenches, and pry bars that are drop-forged instead of cast metal. Casting traps air bubbles in molten metal, creating weak spots.

Price. If in doubt, avoid the most- and least-expensive models. The top end often has more capacity than you need, and the bottom end often has fundamental flaws.

Layout & Prep Tools

You may already have most of the tools needed to lay out a tile project. To square up and level the job, you'll use a level and a square, of course, but you'll also need a chalk-line box to snap guidelines. Where measuring is concerned, take your pick: a measuring tape or a folding carpenter's rule. Not much hammering is involved in tile work, but you may need a hammer (and many other basic tools) to prepare the site—for example, if you have to lay new plywood subflooring. The more prep work you need to do, the more tools you'll need, including a few that will never touch a tile, such as a pipe wrench to loosen fittings in a kitchen or bath.

Remember that tile is hard, and chips can fly when you cut it. Wear safety glasses or goggles to protect your eyes. Because most cutting and grinding procedures create fine dust that can irritate your lungs, wear a respirator or at least a mask during jobs that produce dust. You may also want to invest in a set of knee pads, particularly if you are planning to tile a floor.

A—rubber gloves
B—work gloves
C—knee pads
D—safety glasses
E—safety goggles
F—particle mask
G—respirator
H—ear protectors

A—portable drill
B—level
C—circular saw
D—framing square
E—pipe wrench
F—backer board cutting tool
G—chalk-line box
H—combination square
I—6-in. drywall taping knife
J—measuring tape
K—hammer
L—utility knife
M—sandpaper
N—masonry chisel
O—carpenter's pencil
P—screwdriver
Q—putty knife
R—utility saw

Cutting Tools

To make straight cuts in some glazed tile, all you need is a conventional glass cutter, a metal straightedge, and a length of coat-hanger wire or thin dowel. Simply score the glazed surface of the tile with the cutter guided along the straightedge. Then place the tile on the wire or dowel with the score mark centered directly above it, and press down on both sides of the tile to snap it.

But there are a few improvements that you can easily make on this somewhat simple approach. The most basic is using a snap tile cutter, also called a guillotine cutter because the tool scores and snaps tile. If you have many straight cuts to make, a snap cutter will speed things along considerably and produce cleaner cuts. (Snap cutters are available at tool-rental shops.)

These tools come in several sizes and variations, but most consist of a metal frame that holds the tile in position and a carbide-tipped blade or wheel that travels along a guide rod, ensuring a square cut. Most also have a built-in ridge and a handle that you use to snap the tile once it's scored. After positioning the tile, draw the carbide blade or wheel across the surface to score it. Then press down on the handle until the tile snaps. (See "Using a Snap Tile Cutter," page 46.)

Most snap cutters will not work on large, thick tiles, such as quarry tile or pavers. If you have just a few of these tiles to cut, use this variation of the score-and-snap method. Fit a hacksaw with a carbide-grit blade; then cut a groove about ¹⁄₁₆ inch deep in the face of the tile. (Very thick tiles may require a second cut on the back to get a clean snap.) Then set the tile over a wood dowel or heavy wire, and press down sharply to snap. This system will work but should be reserved for only one or two problem cuts. If you have many tiles proving troublesome to cut in a snap cutter, use a wet saw.

This tool is also the best bet (on any kind of tile) if you have many irregular cuts to make. A wet saw is basically a stationary circular saw with a water-cooled carbide-grit blade. (You can rent one for the job at a tool-rental shop.) The saw component stays put, and you guide the tile into it on a sliding table. (See page 46, **1–3.**)

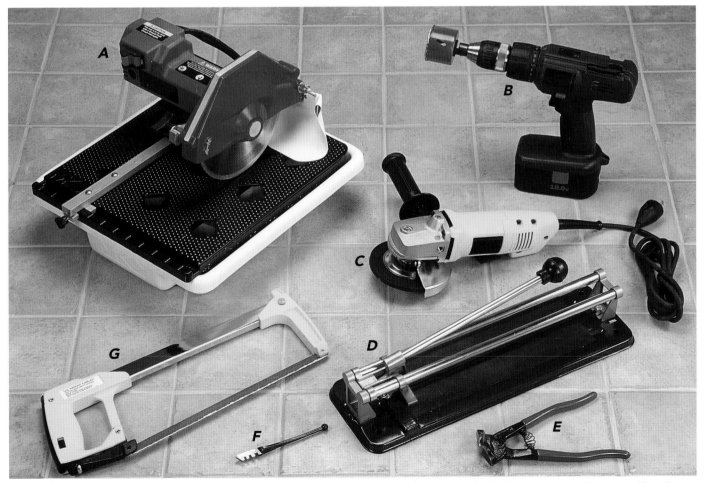

A—wet saw; **B**—cordless drill with carbide hole saw; **C**—handheld grinder with carbide bit; **D**—snap tile cutter; **E**—tile nippers; **F**—glass cutter; **G**—hacksaw with carbide blade

Tile Tip | Using a Snap Tile Cutter

A snap cutter makes quick work of square cuts. Position the tile against the stop at the head of the tool, and draw the scoring wheel across the surface.

The handle on a typical snap cutter has two functions. First use it to score the tile. Then press down to split the tile along the score line.

Using a Wet Saw

Tools and Materials   *Easy*

◆ Wet saw (rentable)

TILE TIP: *Be sure to wear safety glasses when using a wet saw. Also pay particular attention to how you feed the tile into the blade. The tile should be firmly seated on the platform, and you should ease it into the blade, making sure that your fingers stay clear.*

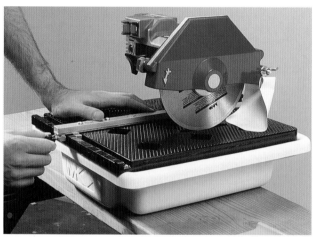

1 A typical wet saw comes fitted to a water reservoir. A circulating system feeds a stream of water onto the cutting area to lubricate the blade.

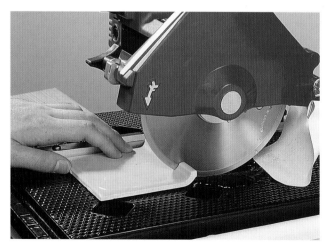

2 On a wet saw, you feed the work into the blade instead of pulling the blade into the work. You need to hold the tile securely on the cutting table.

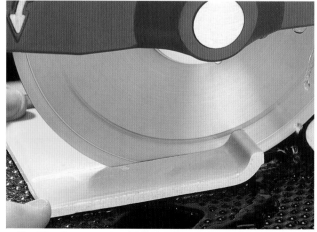

3 The fine-toothed blade slices through tile more slowly than a wood blade cuts through lumber. The saw can handle coves and other shapes.

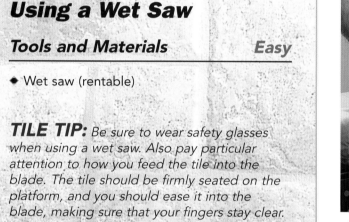

Cutting Irregular Shapes

There are bound to be spots where you can't use a full tile or a partial tile trimmed with a snap cutter. In some cases, you can get by using a straight-cutting tool to slice off a corner. For example, if you are tiling near a base-board convector you may be able to avoid a feed pipe coming through the floor by trimming off a corner of a tile with a snap cutter. The tile may not close up neatly around the pipe, but that won't matter if the cut is concealed by the convector cover.

In many cases, a tile nipper will do the job. The trick is to be patient and take small bites, sometimes as small as ⅛ inch. **1.** Once you get the knack of nibbling away at tiles without cracking them, you'll find that it doesn't take long to fit a tile against a pipe. **2–3.**

Where a pipe will protrude through a tile, instead of nicking its edge, another option is to fit your power drill with a masonry hole saw—a tubular bit with cutting teeth. It's wise to test out a hole-saw cut on scrap tile. You need to hold the drill steady and keep the bit plumb, particularly as you start the cut. The result is a neat hole that allows for grout or caulk. Of course, this approach will work only if you can cut or disconnect the pipe in order to slip the tile in position.

You can also use a wet saw to make irregular cutouts. This tool is particularly handy if you need to fit a tile against molding or any surface with an intricate shape. The idea is to make a series of closely spaced parallel cuts to the required depths. Then break out the thin slices of tile standing between saw kerfs.

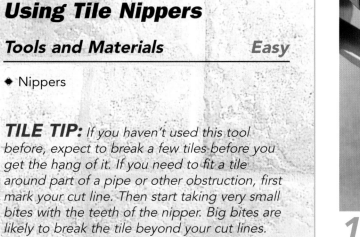

Using Tile Nippers

Tools and Materials   **Easy**

◆ Nippers

TILE TIP: *If you haven't used this tool before, expect to break a few tiles before you get the hang of it. If you need to fit a tile around part of a pipe or other obstruction, first mark your cut line. Then start taking very small bites with the teeth of the nipper. Big bites are likely to break the tile beyond your cut lines.*

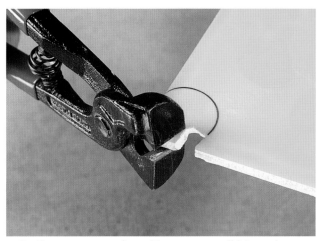

1 Start your cuts by taking very small bites along the edge of the tile. You should work up to your cut marks gradually, which takes patience.

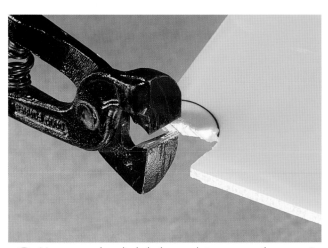

2 You can take slightly larger bites once the area is more defined. It pays to practice on some scrap tiles—and plan for extra waste just in case.

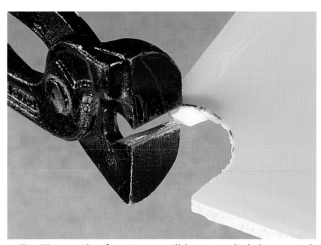

3 The teeth of a nipper will leave a slightly ragged edge. Where appearance counts, you may want to clean up the nipped edges with a file.

Setting Tools & Materials

To set tile, you'll need tools for mixing and spreading adhesive and for embedding and leveling the tiles. You will also need a way to maintain even grout lines. Wall tiles often have spacing nubs molded into their sides. Old-timers sometimes used cotton cord to establish uniform spacing for floor tiles. Some pros are so experienced that they can do the job by eye. But most do-it-yourselfers will find it useful to use plastic spacers.

Mixing & Spreading Adhesive

You should use premixed adhesive on thinset work, and mix your own only in special cases. If you are tackling a thickset mortar job and mixing large amounts of cement-based adhesive, you will need a mason's hoe and wheelbarrow or a large sheet-metal cement-mixing barge. To mix powdered grout, use a bucket and a mortar-mixing paddle or paint mixer chucked in an electric drill. (Use the mixer at a slow speed, 300 rpm or less.)

In most cases, a notched trowel is all you need to apply adhesive. **1–3.** Typically, only one side and one end of the trowel is notched. This allows you to use the flat side to spread the adhesive initially and the notched side to comb out the mix and create even ribs.

Trowels come with various-size square or V-shaped notches for spreading different adhesives for different tiles. The size is specified by the tile or adhesive manufacturer. You may need other mason's tools, such as floats, to level and finish thickset mortar beds.

Spreading Adhesive

Tools and Materials   Easy

- Notched trowel
- Tile adhesive

TILE TIP: Using a notched trowel makes it easy to spread adhesive. You can sweep the blade back and forth and be certain that you are leaving the right amount of adhesive. Just be sure that the depth of the notches on the trowel matches the recommendation of the adhesive manufacturer.

1 Spread adhesive on one section of the floor at a time, not the entire surface, to give yourself some working room on the subfloor surface.

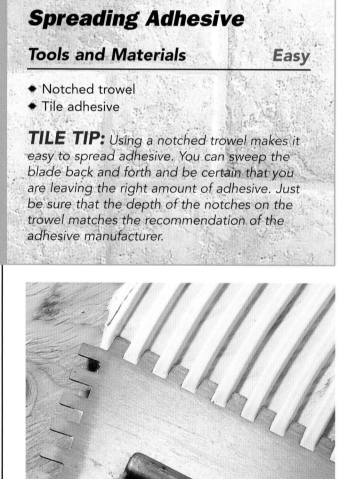

2 Trowel notches produce evenly spaced ribs of adhesive that are the same size. Embed the tiles in the ribs with a slight twist for a secure bond.

3 You can use a sweeping stroke over large areas. First spread out a pile of adhesive before creating the ridges with the toothed edge.

Tile Spacers

To ensure even spacing for grout joints, some tiles (typically wall tiles) have small spacing nubs molded into the edges. When you set two of these tiles together, the nubs match up and create a gap for grout. If the tiles you are using do not have nubs, there are several ways to keep an even layout.

The most reliable system is to set molded plastic spacers in the gaps. **1–2.** These cross-shaped fittings are available in many sizes (generally from ¹⁄₃₂ to ½ inch), so you can use them on small tiles with narrow grout lines and on large tiles with thick grout lines.

Follow the tile manufacturer's recommendations about which size and type to use. Some can be set flat, left in place, and grouted over. Many are set vertically and removed after the tile sets but before you grout.

On countertops, you can mark the centers of the grout lines, attach 6d finishing nails at each end, and stretch dampened cotton cord between them. On floors with wide grout joints, you may want to use wooden battens as spacers.

Embedding & Leveling Tiles

To assist in bedding tiles into adhesive, you may want to use a hammer or rubber mallet and a bedding block. **3.** To make a bedding block, cut a wood block large enough to cover several tiles at once, and cover it with heavy fabric or scrap carpet. You may need a metal straightedge to periodically make sure that the tiles are even and level and that the grout joints remain aligned.

Embedding Tiles

Tools and Materials   *Easy*

- Hammer (or rubber mallet)
- Wood block
- Cushioned cover for block
- Tile spacers

TILE TIP: *You need only moderate pressure over ribs of tile adhesive to create a good bond. But tapping on a padded block that reaches over several tiles may be necessary to be sure that the tiles are flush.*

1 *Moderate pressure combined with a slight side-to-side motion is usually enough to bond the tile with the adhesive.*

2 *Small plastic spacers help to maintain even grout seams as you work tiles into position. You usually remove spacers before grouting.*

3 *Use a piece of 2×4 wrapped in a carpet scrap to even out the tile surface, if necessary. Gentle blows with a hammer provide enough force.*

Finishing Tools

Grout Tools

To apply grout, the typical procedure is to spread a liberal amount across the tile surface, working on a diagonal to the joints with a rubber float or squeegee. With repeated passes you gradually force grout into the joints and compact it.

You can also use a grout bag. It's similar to a pastry bag and has a small fitting on one end to which you can attach nozzles of different sizes to control the amount of grout applied to the joint. After filling the bag, squeeze it to lay a bead of grout directly into the joint. Grout bags work well in situations where cleaning excess grout off the tile surface would be difficult or where the grout might stain the tile surface.

Drawbacks to using the bag include problems with applying a fast-setting grout and mixing this grout to a usable consistency. If the grout is too thin and watery, it won't bond well. If you use the more common method of grouting with a float, it may help if you use a squeegee to clear excess grout off the surface. Then, as the grout dries, you'll need a good sponge or two to remove the grout haze. Rinse the sponge regularly in clean water, and make several passes.

Striking & Jointing Tools

Although most grout is left flush (or nearly flush) to make tile surfaces easier to clean, you may want to strike the grout joints to create a particular pattern. You can buy special striking tools or simply run down the joints with a wooden stick or small tool handle.

Finally, you may need a caulking gun to install polyurethane or silicone caulk in joints where the tile meets dissimilar materials—for example, where wall tiles meet the rim of a tub. Just insert the caulking tube into the gun, snip the tip of the caulking tube, and apply pressure on the gun trigger to fill the gap.

A—masonry trowel; *B*—sponge; *C*—grout sealer with applicator; *D*—bucket; *E*—grout float; *F*—grout bag; *G*—rubber mallet; *H*—scouring pad; *I*—bedding block; *J*—tile spacers; *K*—notched trowel; *L*—carbide emery cloth; *M*—grout saw; *N*—caulking gun; *O*—spacer remover

Basic Materials

Although ceramic tile can be laid over a variety of existing surfaces, there may be cases when you must install a smooth, rigid surface.

Cement Backer Board

Also called cementitious backer units, or CBUs, cement backer board is a rigid, portland cement-based panel designed for use as a substrate or underlayment for ceramic tile in wet or dry areas. Sometimes the binder material is made of fiberglass-reinforced coatings. Different types are recommended for interior floors, interior walls, and exterior walls.

Next to a thick-bed mortar installation, cement backer board is the best substrate for wet areas. Although it is not waterproof, water will not damage it. Wood, plywood, particleboard, and drywall underlayments will deteriorate when exposed to water. And because cement backer board is a rigid, dense, dimensionally stable product, it does not expand and contract as much as conventional wood subflooring and underlayment materials.

Backer board is available in several thicknesses. The most commonly used is ½-inch thick. The panels also come in several widths, but are usually 4 × 4 or 3 × 5 feet.

You install CBUs basically the same way you install drywall. The panels are a bit trickier to cut, but you can score and snap the panels to get a clean edge. Because CBUs are heavy and rigid, install them directly over wall studs using corrosion-resistant nails or screws.

Backer board is also fireproof, so you can use it in place of asbestos board as an insulating material for woodstove surrounds. And using it in conjunction with tile may allow reduced clearances between the stove and wall. Check the manufacturer's directions and local building codes to be sure of clearances at combustion sources.

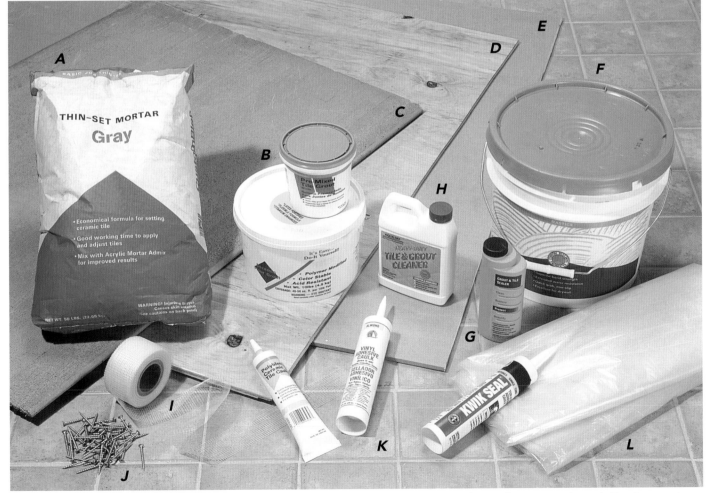

A—thinset mortar mix; *B*—premixed tile grouts; *C*—cement backer board; *D*—plywood; *E*—greenboard; *F*—tile mastic; *G*—tile & grout sealer; *H*—tile and grout cleaner; *I*—fiberglass mesh tape; *J*—galvanized screws; *K*—caulking products; *L*—4-mil plastic film (waterproof membrane)

Waterproof & Isolation Membranes

To make a tile job durable, you need to keep out water, which can weaken the bond between the tile and underlayment and eventually damage the underlayment and framing beneath. In a wet area such as a tub surround, waterproof membranes are recommended between the studs and the substrate to prevent this kind of damage.

It's tempting sometimes to use waterproof membranes when you want to install tile over concrete floors that are subject to rising water from below. But the best plan in such cases is to deal with whatever is causing the problem, such as faulty drainage. Tar paper or building felt have long been used as moisture-resistant membranes. Other types include chlorinated polyethylene

(generally called CPE) and combination liquid and fabric membranes. Make sure the membrane is compatible with the setting material.

Isolation membranes separate tile from the underlayment to compensate for differences in expansion and contraction rates of the dissimilar materials. Typically, they consist of chlorinated polyethylene sheets laminated between the tile and substrate. You may need an isolation membrane if the existing underlayment shows signs of excessive movement. Signs include cracks in masonry and cracks at joints where two different subflooring materials meet. If you suspect excessive seasonal movement or a weak substructure, it's best to seek professional advice.

Expansion Joints

Place expansion joints around installations where tile abuts a different material. When tiling a floor, simply stop the tile and underlayment about ¼ inch short of the wall, and fill the joint with a flexible silicone caulk. Prefabricated PVC corner expansion joints are also available. On interior walls and floors, special joints are usually not needed within the tile field itself. Filling all joints between field tiles with the appropriate grout should provide the proper cohesive bond.

You may need control joints on large patios, where the joints are needed about every 16 feet. You make control joints by pulling a special tool across the uncured concrete, leaving a groove. Designed to be the weak link in the concrete slab, control joints should crack. These joints in the substrate are generally carried up through the grout lines between the surface tiles. You can fill these joints with a compressible foam rod topped by urethane caulk instead of a traditional grout.

Interior Application

Exterior Application

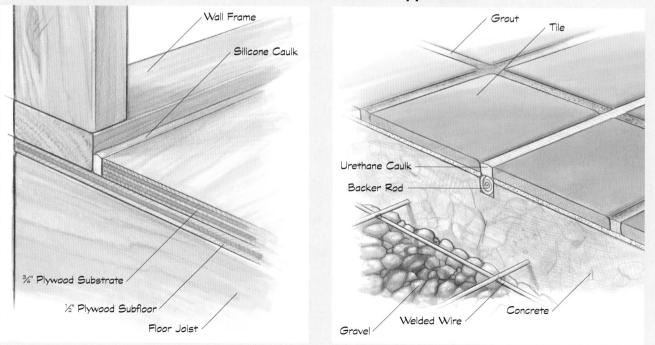

Mortar & Adhesives

The traditional setting method is to lay the tiles directly in a bed of wet portland cement mortar. It's still used in some situations—for example, if you need to create a sloping floor in a shower enclosure. But most tile work is done with thinset adhesive.

Thickset

Installing thick-bed mortar requires considerable experience. Some tile-setters lay down the mortar bed, smooth it, allow it to cure, and then set the tiles over the bed with a bond coat of cement adhesive. In any case, the job is best left to a professional.

Thinset

There are many thinset adhesives on the market. A tile dealer can recommend the best adhesive for the job, but you will probably wind up using a cement-based adhesive (mortar) or an organic mastic adhesive, and in some cases an epoxy-based mortar.

Portland Cement Mortars

These adhesives are actually forms of cement-based mortar, although they should not be confused with the portland cement mortar used for thick-bed installations.

Most of these nonflammable, thinset mortars come in powder form. Some must be mixed with sand before use. Some come as premixed liquids. Powdered forms are mixed with water or a liquid latex additive.

Dry-Set Mortars

These are the most common adhesives, generally sold in powder form and mixed with water. Highly resistant to impact, dry-set mortar can be cleaned up easily with water. Once cured, this mortar is not affected by prolonged contact with water, so it can be used in wet installations.

A typical installation has a layer about $\frac{3}{32}$ inch thick. The material will cover and level minor surface irregularities, but it is not intended as a setting bed or for leveling very rough surfaces.

Dry-set mortars adhere well to a variety of substrate materials, including relatively smooth masonry, insulation board, drywall, and cement backer board. Some types are suitable for use over plywood. Check the label for appropriate applications.

Latex Portland Cement Mortars

These mortars are a mixture of portland cement, sand, and a liquid latex additive. They have the same basic applications as dry-set mortars, although they have

Setting Alternatives

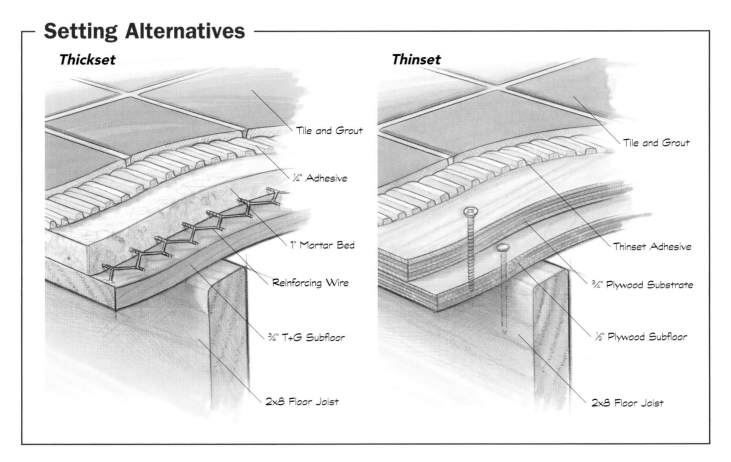

Thickset

Tile and Grout
¼" Adhesive
1" Mortar Bed
Reinforcing Wire
¾" T+G Subfloor
2x8 Floor Joist

Thinset

Tile and Grout
Thinset Adhesive
¾" Plywood Substrate
½" Plywood Subfloor
2x8 Floor Joist

higher compressive and bond strengths and greater flexibility. Latex portland cement mortars cost a bit more than the dry-set kind, but they perform better.

Organic Mastic Adhesives

Although most of these adhesives do not have the bond strength or leveling properties of thinsets, they are the easiest to apply. Most brands cannot be used in wet installations or near heat sources, however. (Organic adhesives generally should not be used in areas with temperatures over 140 degrees F.) Suitable backings include drywall, smooth plaster or mortar, plywood, tile backer board, and smooth, dry concrete. Organic mastics are water-based.

Epoxy-Based Mortars

Epoxies are not used much by do-it-yourselfers because they are more expensive and harder to apply than other adhesives. You must mix the resin and hardener to exact proportions and apply them at the correct temperature to ensure the right setting time and pot life. Epoxy mortars are useful when you need a high degree of bond strength or when the tiled surface will receive a high degree of physical or chemical wear. They will adhere to just about any substrate material.

Grouts & Sealers

Grouts

Tile grouts fall into two basic categories: cement-based grout and epoxy grout. Don't confuse grouts used for tiling with caulks, which are used for filling gaps between building materials. For example, silicone caulk is used at joints where tile meets other surfaces. And because silicone is highly flexible, you can use it instead of grout at tiled corners and edges where movement in the substructure would crack ordinary grout joints. It's also good practice to caulk the joint between wall tiles and a tub.

Cement-Based Grouts. These grouts have a base of portland cement, but they differ in the types of additives they contain. Coloring pigments are available for many of them, although precolored grouts also are sold.

Most cement-based grouts come in powdered form to which water or liquid latex is added. Some grouts are premixed and ready to use, but they are usually the most expensive as well. Cement-based grouts include commercial portland cement, dry-set, and latex portland cement grouts.

Tile Tip · Sealing Grout

Glazed tiles have great resistance to dirt, mold, and mildew. But the grout between tiles can become a chronic cleaning problem unless you protect it with a sealer. Mildew can be removed using bleach. Ground-in dirt on floors and such may be impossible to remove. Here you should use dark grouts.

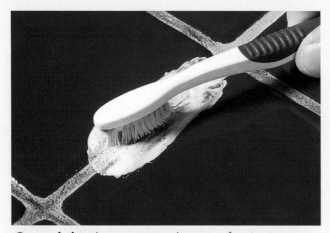

General cleaning may not take care of stains in grout. Try to scrub the grout using a brush (even an old toothbrush) with a concentrated cleaner and/or bleach.

To protect grout seams in areas that are chronically damp or exposed to traffic, use a small brush to coat cleaned grout with a liberal coat of liquid silicone sealer.

Portland Cement Grout. A mixture of portland cement and other ingredients, this grout produces a dense, uniformly colored material. Like all cement-based mortars, it is resistant to water but not completely waterproof or stainproof, so it generally requires a sealer. Commercial portland cement grouts are formulated for use with thick-bed portland cement mortar installations. With these, you need to soak the tiles in water before application. These grouts also require damp-curing to prevent shrinking and cracking.

Dry-Set Grout. This type of portland cement grout contains additives that increase water-retention. They allow you to grout tiles without presoaking them and without damp-curing the grout once applied. If you are grouting the tiles on a hot, dry day, the grout might dry out so quickly that it will shrink, requiring you to presoak tiles and damp-cure the grout joints anyway.

Latex Portland Cement Grout. This can be any of the preceding grout types that have been mixed with powdered latex and water, or with liquid latex instead of water. This versatile grout is somewhat stronger and more flexible than latex cement mortar.

Epoxy Grout. This grout contains an epoxy resin and hardener, giving it a high degree of chemical resistance, bond strength, and impact resistance. It is the most expensive grout, and therefore usually confined to commercial applications where chemical resistance is required. Epoxy grout generally flows more easily than standard grout and is somewhat more difficult to apply. If your tiles are more than ½ inch thick and the grout joints are less than ¼ inch wide, the grout may not penetrate.

Sealers

Clear liquid tile and grout sealers provide protection against stains and, to some extent, against water penetration at grout joints. Their application is the final step in tile installation. Although glazed tiles themselves do not require a sealer, the cement-based grout joints usually do because they are more porous than tile. Most sealers have a silicone, lacquer, or acrylic base. Different formulations are available for different types of tile and grout in various applications. Sealers generally require reapplication every one to two years to maintain protection. But they can reduce the formation of mold and mildew in grouted joints.

Grout Types

Tile/Application	Commercial Portland Cement		Sand Portland Cement	Dry-Set	Latex Portland Cement (1)	Epoxy (2, 3)	Silicone or Urethane (4)	Modified Epoxy Emulsion (1, 3)
	Walls	Floors	Walls & Floors	Walls & Floors				
Glazed Wall Tile (More than 7% absorption)	✔			✔	✔		✔	
Ceramic Mosaic Tile	✔	✔	✔	✔	✔	✔	✔	✔
Quarry, Paver, & Packing House Tile	✔	✔	✔			✔		✔
Dry or Limited Water Exposure	✔	✔	✔	✔	✔	✔	✔	✔
Wet Areas	✔	✔	✔	✔	✔	✔	✔	✔
Exteriors	✔	✔	✔	✔	✔(5)	✔(5)		✔(5)
Stain Resistance (6)	D	C	E	D	B	A	A	B
Crack Resistance (6)	D	D	E	D	C	B	A Flexible	C
Colorability (6)	B	B	C	B	B	B	Restricted	B

(1) Special cleaning procedures and materials needed.
(2) Mainly used for chemical-resistant properties.
(3) Epoxies are recommended for prolonged temperatures up to 140°F, high-temperature-resistant epoxies up to 350°F.
(4) Special tools needed for proper application. Silicone
and urethane are used when installing pregrouted ceramic tile sheets. Silicone grout should not be used on kitchen countertops or other food-preparation surfaces.
(5) Follow manufacturer's directions.
(6) Five performance ratings—best to minimal (A B C D E).

CHAPTER 3

...

TILING FLOORS

On floors, ceramic and stone tiles provide a durable surface that will complement practically any room and its furnishings. Bear in mind, though, that tile can be hard and cold underfoot. That's why it is not often used in bedrooms or living rooms, and reserved mainly for kitchens, baths, and entry halls.

Before you lay a ceramic or stone tile floor, the existing floor must be strong and rigid enough to support the added weight of the tile. Strength is rarely a problem because residential floors generally are built to carry at least 40 pounds per square foot—more than enough to carry tile. But you may need to strengthen joists or add extra subflooring (or both) to make the floor rigid enough that it does not flex.

The work area must also be reasonably square for the installation to look good. There are extreme cases (mainly in older homes) where a floor covering with a nondirectional pattern such as carpeting might look better than a grid pattern of tile. But you usually can deal with minor discrepancies by adjusting the tile layout to visually de-emphasize the condition.

Design Basics

Although the subject of design involves numerous considerations—and is largely a matter of personal taste—a few basic principles always apply.

When choosing a tile for your floor, you need to consider five elements: size, shape, color, texture, and pattern. Together, all five elements determine the overall visual effect you are trying to achieve. The first four elements apply to the tile you select. The last element, pattern, is controlled both by the tile itself and by the way they are arranged on the floor.

Size

As a general rule, tile size has an inverse effect on rooms: small tiles make a floor look larger, and large tiles make a floor look smaller. If you're tiling a small lavatory with several twists and turns in the walls, a small, simple, and uniform tile will probably look best. If you're tiling a somewhat cavernous entry hall at the foot of a expansive two-story stairwell, 12×12s may help to pull the large space together.

But there is always a trade-off in design decisions. Where tile size is concerned, it involves both installation time and possible future maintenance. Because large tiles cover a lot of area, installing them is faster than it would be with small tiles. Also, there are fewer grout lines in a field of large tiles, which means less cleaning and sealing as the floor is subjected to daily wear and tear.

Tile size *should be appropriate for the room, with larger units and size combinations reserved for large spaces.*

Tile shapes *(and different surface textures) can be combined to create borders and define areas.*

Shape

Because most tiles are square, this is the shape people expect to see. When you choose a different shape (hexagonal, octagonal, or ogee, for instance) or combine shapes such as squares and rectangles, you immediately draw attention to the floor.

Color

Dark colors tend to make a space look smaller, while lighter shades generally provide a more spacious feeling. Warm terra-cotta colors suggest a rustic look, whereas black, white, and bold colors can impart a more modern appearance. Light pastels, such as pink, peach, or light blues and greens, can soften a room while lending an airy feeling. Sharply contrasting colors and patterns usually draw attention to the floor, whereas a single-color or low-contrast color scheme creates a subtle backdrop for furniture or other focal points in the room. You need to plan color schemes carefully, considering wall paint color, natural light, and other factors, to avoid conflicts with other elements in the room.

Tile color *can be uniform but still vary slightly to provide highlights and tie together a large entry area.*

Texture

The surface texture of a tile often plays a more subtle role than the other style elements. But it is an important link to the overall feeling of a room with a tiled floor. For example, handmade Mexican pavers have an uneven surface that creates a purposefully irregular, heavily textured look. Combined with color gradations within each tile, this can set a distinctly rustic style. On the other hand, machine-made pavers with a uniformly smooth surface texture and even coloring have a crisp, clean look. A highly glazed surface can seem to expand a space and brighten a room, while a matte finish often diminishes space and makes a room feel more cozy.

Pattern

The way you combine the different design elements of shape, size, and color determines the overall pattern of the floor. Consider that the pattern serves not only to add visual interest to the floor but also can underscore particular features of a room, such as its length. A strong directional pattern running lengthwise makes a room look longer and narrower, while a crossing pattern makes a room look shorter and wider. You can also use multiple patterns to define areas. For example, you might change a square grid layout in the main field into a diagonal pattern around the edge of a room or along a walkway. A pattern change can also

Tile texture *as well as size and shape can help to define walkways, entries, and other areas of a room.*

Tile patterns *range from a subtle contrasting shade in a border to highly defined murals and mosaics.*

separate spaces—at a pass-through between rooms, for example—while a continuing grid serves to draw them together. Manipulating lines of sight can also increase apparent space and create a unifying effect—for instance, when you continue tile from inside onto an outdoor patio. Generally, busy patterns decrease apparent floor size, while simple patterns enlarge it.

Grout has an impact on the design. Using a contrasting grout color will emphasize a pattern, while a matching grout color provides a more subtle effect. Remember that dark grout hides dirt better than a light color, so think twice before using white grout. If you also plan on tiling the wall, it is usually best to use one size of tile on the wall and another on the floor, especially if floors and walls are not perfectly level, square, or plumb.

Changing scale or pattern—installing what amounts to a tile baseboard, for example—will separate wall and floor grids and disguise any discrepancies where grout joints might not align. There are many types of specially shaped tiles, generally with a cove shape, that suit this purpose. Also, you can include a strip of border tiles of a contrasting color or pattern around the room perimeter to frame a pattern in the main tile field. Be sure to subtract the thickness of the cove when planning the layout of the field tiles on the floor.

Even within these basic guidelines there are so many possibilities that it pays to experiment before you decide on a final combination of elements. You can do this on your own with graph paper and colored pencils, or use the computer-imaging services available at some tile stores and home centers.

Finish

For indoor floors, you can use a glazed or unglazed tile. Glazed tiles are easier to clean, while some unglazed tiles require sealing and waxing. If you want to use an unglazed tile indoors, use a vitreous quarry tile that is at least somewhat stain resistant. In wet areas, choose a tile with a slip-resistant surface, and avoid slick, highly glazed tiles. Outdoors, unglazed tiles are often a better choice than tiles with a glazed surface, which can be slick when wet.

Also, consider investing some extra time in the job of finishing the grout, particularly in damp areas where mildew forms easily on the surface. A protective coat of clear silicone, for example, can make cleaning and maintenance much easier.

You can combine tiles *of different colors, sizes, patterns, and textures into a unique design.*

Planning the Layout

The best approach is to plan the tile layout on paper. A scale drawing will enable you to visualize what the installation will look like before you start, and help you estimate the number of tiles you need. It also corrects any layout problems in advance, before you establish working lines on the floor itself.

Check for Square. In small rooms, you can usually check the squareness with a framing square positioned at each corner of the room. For larger rooms, you can use the 3-4-5 triangle method. Measure 3 feet along one wall and 4 feet on the other; the distance between the points should equal 5 feet if the corner is square. **1.** In very large rooms, you might want to double the ratio (6-8-10) for greater accuracy. If the floor is less than ⅛ inch out of square in 10 feet, you can usually compensate for the condition by adjusting the working lines according to the pattern in which you will be laying the tile. If one wall is well out of square, plan the layout so that the tapered tiles are positioned along the least noticeable wall in the room.

Check for Level. Use a spirit level to check the floor along each wall. **2–3.** An out-of-level floor does not present serious problems unless you plan to extend the tile up the wall. If this is the case, consider using a continuous baseboard and a different type of wallcovering.

Check for Wavy Walls. Even if the walls are reasonably square, they may be bowed or wavy, which also may be noticeable when the tile is installed. **4–5.** If this con-

dition is not already apparent from inspection of the existing floor covering, you can often detect a bowed or wavy condition by simply sighting down the wall at floor level. You can also snap a chalk line on the floor parallel with the wall and take measurements at various points. In extreme cases, you may want to remove the wall material and shim out the studs to correct the condition.

Make a Scale Drawing. A scale drawing will help you lay out and estimate the tile job. Be sure to indicate the locations of entryways and any built-in cabinets or other permanent fixtures. Measure the size of the tile itself and the width of one full grout joint, and use this as the basic measuring unit.

If you are using square tiles, plan your drawing so that each square on the graph paper represents one tile and its grout-joint measurement. If your tile is rectangular and its proportions will permit, allow one square to equal the small dimension and two squares to equal the long dimension. You also can lay down two or more tiles to create a square dimension. The idea is to superimpose a field of tiles on an outline of the room to see how it fits. You can try many different plans on an overlay of tracing paper, using colored pencils to help you visualize what the pattern will look like.

Plan the layout so a narrow row of cut tiles does not end up in a visually conspicuous place, such as at a doorway or entry. Often, the best plan is to adjust the field so that cut tiles at opposite sides of the room will be the same size. This gives the most symmetrical look to the installation. If you start by laying a full row of tiles along one wall, you sometimes end up with a narrow row of partial tiles along the opposite wall. It can be

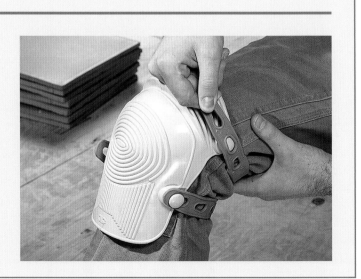

Checking for Square and Level

Tools and Materials 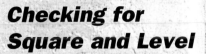 Easy

- Measuring tape
- Level and straightedge
- String and blocks

TILE TIP: *Few corners are exactly square, and few floors are dead level, particularly in older homes. But you can make most of these problems disappear by making very minor adjustments in the tile field of grouted joints.*

1 Use the proportions of a 3-4-5 right triangle to check corners for square. With legs of 3 and 4 ft., the diagonal is 5 ft. if the corner is square.

2 Use a 4-ft. spirit level to check the floor across corners. Checking for level is even more important if you are adding wall tile.

3 Set the level on a long, straight 2x4 (or strip of plywood) to read level over a larger area. Swivel the board around to find high and low spots.

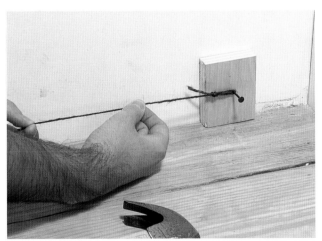

4 Use blocks and string to check the wall for straightness. Start by mounting a block of wood at each corner. Then stretch a string between them.

5 To check for flatness, use a third block the same thickness as the other two to check the gap between the string and wall at several locations.

difficult to eliminate the narrow row by adjusting the width of grout joints.

Similarly, if you start laying tiles from the exact center of the room out toward each wall, you may end up with narrow cut tiles at both walls. To correct this, shift the original centerline, or working line, a distance equal to half a tile to the left or right. This will give you wider-cut tiles at both walls. Also, try to center the tiles across large openings, such as archways, or beneath focal points, such as picture windows or fireplaces, especially if the tiles are large. If the tiles extend into an adjacent room, lay out both floors so that the grout joints line up through the entryways.

In short, if you plan the layout carefully in advance on paper, you will eliminate unpleasant surprises once the project is well underway. Remember, once even a few tiles are set in adhesive, it becomes very difficult to make changes in the overall layout.

Irregular Tiles. A careful layout is even more important if you are using tiles with irregular shapes. They are generally sold by the square foot, so it is easy to get a rough estimate of how many you'll need. But for a more accurate estimate, you can lay out a few tiles with spaced grout joints to see how these more complicated shapes will fall along the edges of the room. The main concern, of course, is all the extra cutting that will be required where irregular shapes meet a boundary.

If you plan to use handmade tile or any material that does not have a uniform size, the basic layout rules still apply. But you will likely have to make small adjustments in the grout seams to make a balanced installation.

Basic Tile Shapes and Patterns

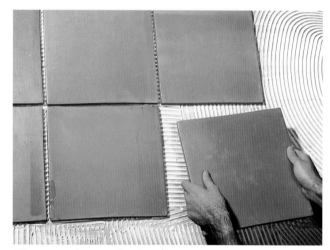

The most basic tile shape is a square that forms a symmetrical grid, such as 12 x 12 terra-cotta.

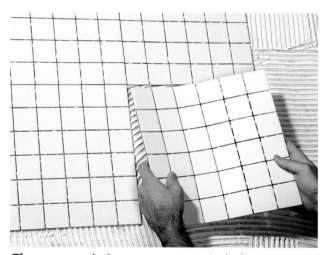

The many variations on a square include sizes you set individually and the sheet-mounted tile shown.

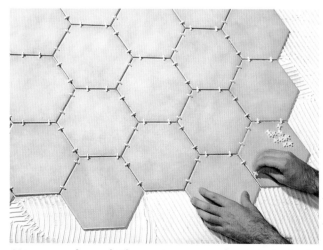

Hexagon-shaped tile creates more of an interlocked, multidirectional pattern, and requires edge trimming.

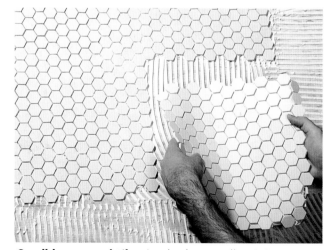

Small hexagonal tiles (and other small units) are sheet-mounted to make installation more convenient.

Tile Tip   Making a Layout Stick

A layout stick with marks for tile and grout can come in handy when you establish working lines on the floor. It's also good for spacing tiles if you don't use spacers. The stick can be a straight piece of 1x4 (for ¾-inch tile), cut to 3 or 4 feet if you're working in a small batch or up to 8 feet on larger rooms.

    If you're using individual tiles or tiles with lugs on the edges to control grout spacing, mark the dimensions of the tile and joints along the edge of the stick. With tile sheets, mark the size of the sheets, leaving spaces for the joints between each sheet.

Align tiles *with lugs to create the proper spacing; then use a combination square to transfer marks to the layout stick.*

Rectangular tiles can form many patterns, *from straight running bonds to basketweaves.*

By combining basic shapes *such as squares and rectangles, you can create a wide variety of patterns.*

Sheet-mounted tiles *are available in many patterns, including random combinations of color and size.*

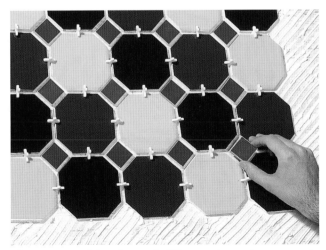

Custom combinations *of different sizes, shapes, and colors are possible if you stick to stock sizes.*

Preparing the Floor

Tiling is no different from other do-it-yourself projects in one important respect: much of the work involved (and often the key to a successful project) lies in the preparation. The main concern, of course, is strength. To support tile and grout without flexing enough to cause cracking, the floor must be stronger than a typical floor. It can't flex. This can make a tile floor somewhat less comfortable than a wood floor.

You can install ceramic tile directly over many existing floor coverings if the floor covering itself and the subflooring and framing below are sound. If the existing floor meets these requirements—for example, the plywood floor under carpeting—thoroughly clean the floor and, if necessary, roughen the existing surface with sandpaper to ensure a good adhesive bond. It's also a good idea to check the surface for raised seams and popped nailheads. The seams you can reduce with a block plane. The popped nails you can deal with two ways: drive them home, or pull them out and drive screws instead.

The added thickness of tile will cause a change of floor level, which will have to be dealt with at entryways where the tile meets other floor coverings. You may have to trim narrow strips off the bottoms of doors as well.

In many cases, an existing floor structure will require some tear-out and rebuilding. In some houses, you may have to remove the surface flooring, strip some of the subflooring, build up some of the framing, and start

To support heavy tiles and prevent cracking, you generally need extra subflooring and sometimes extra framing, too.

from scratch. In many cases, adding one extra layer of plywood will do.

If you find that it is too difficult to remove an old floor covering, and it is in bad shape, you may be able to bury it under plywood or a backer-board underlayment and make a sound surface for new tile.

New Construction

If you are working with new floor construction, plan the job to provide extra-strength framing and subflooring for tiled areas. If a standard floor in the house has 2×8s covered with ½-inch plywood sheathing, there are two approaches you could take to build in extra strength: increase the joist size or decrease the joist spacing. You could switch to 2×10s or, if there is not enough room

for the extra depth, decrease the spacing between joist centers from the standard 16 inches to 12 inches.

As for subflooring, you could leave the existing ½-inch panels in place and cover them with another layer of ½- or ⅝- or even ¾-inch-thick plywood. There are also special-order floor systems that provide exceptional strength. These include I-beam wood joists, and 1-inch-thick plywood panels milled with overlapping edges. It generally pays to install the plywood using screws instead of nails; they provide more holding power.

If you install an extra layer of subflooring (as most jobs require either extra plywood or cement-based backer board), avoid aligning seams with the existing material. Joints between panels on the different layers should bear on different floor joists.

Strengthening the Subfloor

Tools and Materials   Moderate

- Drill with screwdriver bit and screws
- Level
- Extra joist
- Construction adhesive

TILE TIP: *Remember that wooden floors are resilient; they flex a bit when you walk on them. But to support tile without cracking, you need to eliminate the flexing as much as possible.*

1 An extra layer of plywood (generally ½ in. thick or more) solidifies the floor. Screws provide more holding power than nails in old and new layers.

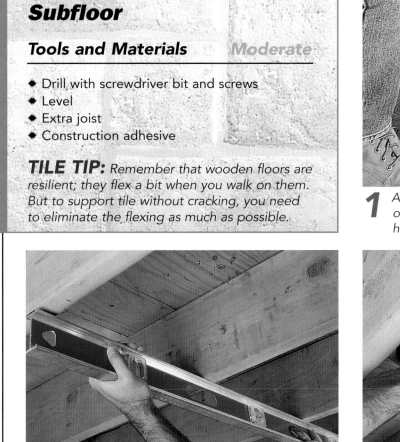

2 Locate a weak or sagging joist by checking across several joists with a level. It will rock over the lowest one where the floor dips.

3 Strengthen a weak joist (after propping it up if need be) by adding a second joist secured with construction adhesive and screws.

Reinforcing the Subfloor

If an existing floor feels spongy or excessively flexible when you walk on it—or if it squeaks over a large area—chances are that you will need to reinforce it. If the floor sags noticeably, you will need to level it.

Start by renailing or screwing the subfloor to the floor joists. If you have an older, board-type subfloor, you can shim individual loose boards with shingles. Gently tap shims into the space between the joists and the subfloor to prevent movement. Do not drive the shims too forcefully, or they will cause the boards to rise, resulting in a wavy floor. Then nail or screw the boards to the joists.

If several boards are loose or a sagging joist has created a springy spot in a plywood subfloor, you can add a cleat beside or between the joists in question. For example, you can cut a short piece of wood the same depth as the joists, coat its top with construction adhesive, tap it into place between joists (under the weak area), and nail it securely.

If a large area of the entire subfloor is weak because joists have settled or shifted, one approach is to strengthen the floor by adding wood or metal bridging.

You can also double up weak joists after propping them up temporarily with posts.

Make sure the existing subfloor material itself is in good shape. It should be sound, even, and level. In bathrooms especially, water damage to the subfloor might not be apparent until you remove the finish flooring. Replace all rotted or water-damaged wood. If a subfloor is simply wet but still sound, allow it to dry thoroughly before tiling over it. Fix the problem causing the wetness to prevent future problems.

Typically, the total thickness of the subfloor, underlayment, and existing floor material (if retained) should be at least $1\frac{1}{8}$ inches thick. If it is not, build up the subfloor by adding an additional layer of exterior plywood (CDX or better grade), or use cement-based backer board. It is recommended for wet areas. Do not use interior-grade plywood, particleboard, or hardboard.

Underlayment

You will also need to install an underlayment of plywood or backer board over wood-board subfloors, because flexing between individual boards can crack tile or grout joints. Such underlayment can also be used to

---

Bridging

Bridging is short blocks of wood or strips of metal set between floor joists. It connects the joists to each other and can prevent twisting where the bottom edges are left exposed—for example, over a crawl space. There are two basic types of bridging: wood and metal. Wood bridging can be solid pieces of lumber set perpendicularly between the joists, or smaller pieces of lumber set in an X-shape. Metal bridging uses two strips of steel in an X pattern. Although bridging may not be required by building codes in your floor, most people find that it adds a noticeable degree of stiffness and strength.

To install metal bridging, you mount the nailing flange on the edge of the joist. You can't use these on existing floors without bending down the top flanges.

Solid bridging is easy to install because you use short lengths of lumber the same size as the floor joists. A staggered pattern allows you to end-nail each piece.

provide a smooth, level surface over an uneven subfloor. Both types of underlayment should be at least ½ inch thick, no matter what the thickness of the subflooring.

If you plan to install a new subfloor directly over the joists, use two layers, one of at least ⅝-inch exterior plywood (¾-inch is even better), the second of ½-inch exterior plywood or backer board. Check local building codes for guidance.

With plywood, allow a ⅛-inch gap between each sheet and about ¼ inch where sheets meet adjoining walls to allow for expansion and contraction. **1–2.** Attach the plywood to the existing subflooring with construction adhesive and 6d ring-shank nails or 1¼-inch galvanized, all-purpose (drywall-type) screws. **3.** If you are using backer board, consult the manufacturer's literature for

recommended installation methods. Generally, the boards are embedded in thinset. Drive nails or screws around the panel perimeter about ½ inch in from the edge and 6 inches on center. Then drive fasteners across the face of the panel in rows about 16 inches on center, spacing them 8 to 12 inches apart.

Make sure the heads are set below the surface to avoid stress points that can crack tiles. Joints between backer board panels are typically filled with tile-setting adhesive and taped with fiberglass mesh tape. Fill the joints between plywood panels with floor-patch compound, wood putty, or tile-setting adhesive. After installing the underlayment, sand any rough or splintery surfaces, and make sure the surface is clean and free of debris before installing the tile.

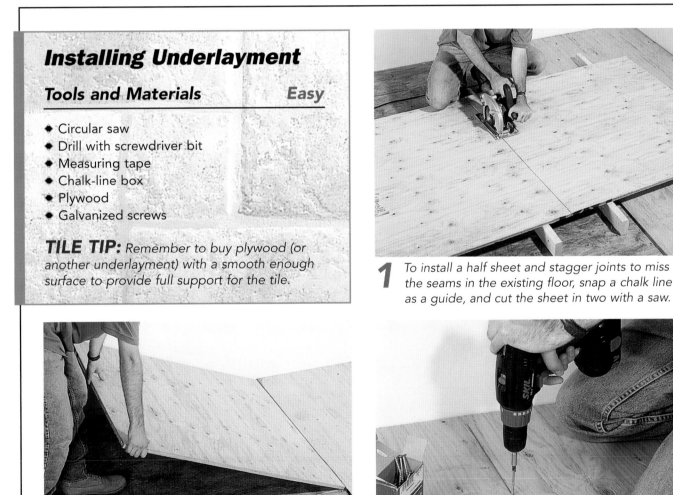

Installing Underlayment

Tools and Materials   Easy

- Circular saw
- Drill with screwdriver bit
- Measuring tape
- Chalk-line box
- Plywood
- Galvanized screws

TILE TIP: Remember to buy plywood (or another underlayment) with a smooth enough surface to provide full support for the tile.

1 To install a half sheet and stagger joints to miss the seams in the existing floor, snap a chalk line as a guide, and cut the sheet in two with a saw.

2 Set a half sheet next to a full sheet to stagger the seams. Leave at least a ¼-in. gap between the edges of the sheets and the walls.

3 Drive screws long enough to reach through the old and new floors. Snap a line so you drive them into supporting joists.

Tiling Over Concrete

In theory, there is no better subfloor for tile than a concrete slab. It has no flex at all, unlike a wood-framed floor, and provides the kind of stable base needed to keep grout seams from cracking. But on some slabs, you may need to do some repair work to create a smooth and level surface.

If there is a fault in the floor, for example, you need to patch it. Start by chipping away any loose or ragged edges with a hammer and cold chisel. (You need to wear eye protection because chips can fly up with great force.) Then prepare the fault for patching by brushing out the dust and debris, and dampening it. Another option is to apply a liquid bonding agent that helps cement stick in the patch area. Fill the crack with

cement, and smooth out the surface with a trowel. You should be able to get by with only one coat.

For old concrete slabs that are in good shape structurally, remove any dirt or residue with a mild detergent. Avoid using harsh chemical cleaners such as concrete and driveway cleaning solutions. They may leave a residue that interferes with the adhesive bond.

Allow new concrete floors or walls to cure for at least one month before you install the tile. If a form-release agent or acceleration compound was used on the concrete, it could interfere with a good adhesive bond. If water beads up on the surface rather than being absorbed, it's likely that chemicals have been used. If so, you may have to install an underlayment to be certain of good tile adhesion.

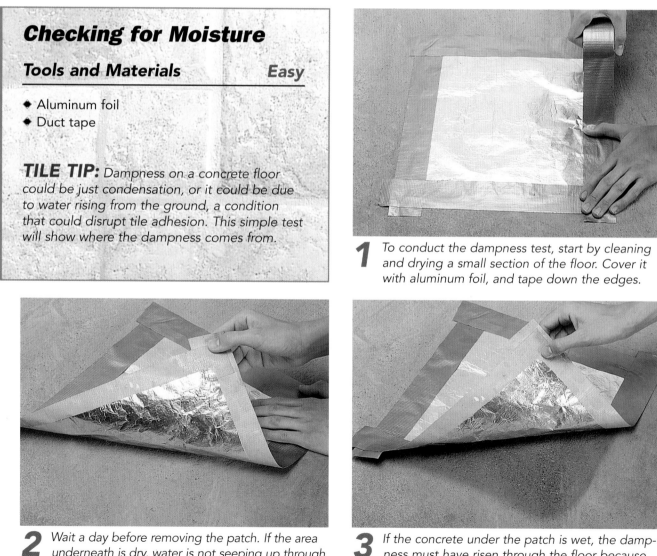

Checking for Moisture

Tools and Materials   **Easy**

- Aluminum foil
- Duct tape

TILE TIP: Dampness on a concrete floor could be just condensation, or it could be due to water rising from the ground, a condition that could disrupt tile adhesion. This simple test will show where the dampness comes from.

1 To conduct the dampness test, start by cleaning and drying a small section of the floor. Cover it with aluminum foil, and tape down the edges.

2 Wait a day before removing the patch. If the area underneath is dry, water is not seeping up through the floor; the dampness is from condensation.

3 If the concrete under the patch is wet, the dampness must have risen through the floor because the foil stopped condensation from forming.

Preparing Concrete Floors

Tools and Materials   *Easy*

- Masonry hammer and cold chisel
- Brush
- Mason's and concrete finishing trowels
- Cement patch
- Gloves

TILE TIP: *To get the best bond with patch material, use the chisel to slightly undercut the top edges of the crack.*

1 Use a cold chisel and a masonry hammer to chip away rough edges of the crack. Deepen shallow areas so that the patch material gets a good hold.

2 Brush out dust and debris, which can decrease adhesion. You may want to dampen the crack or add a bonding agent before troweling in cement.

3 Use a trowel to fill the crack. Cement will do, although one variety, called hydraulic cement, swells slightly as it sets to make a tight bond.

4 Fill minor depressions in a concrete slab with flash-patch material. Spread it with a trowel the way you would spread drywall compound on a wall.

5 Smooth out the patch area using a large trowel that can ride on the finished floor. You can feather flash-patch compound to a fine edge.

Installing Floor Tiles

To keep the first rows straight, snap chalk lines along the floor. Work adhesive up to your guidelines using a notched trowel, but don't apply more adhesive than you can cover with tile before the adhesive skins over or sets up. The amount of workable area depends both on the working time of the adhesive and on the speed at which you lay the tiles. Start with a small area, and work up to larger areas as your speed increases. **1–3.**

When you spread the adhesive, use the method and notch size recommended by the tile dealer. Be careful not to cover the working lines with adhesive. For extra-thick tile or tile that has a deep-ridged back pattern, butter the back side with adhesive as well as the floor.

After spreading the adhesive, press a tile into place and twist it slightly—to bed it firmly. You can also use a bedding block to ensure that tiles in a field are flat and firmly embedded. Slide the block (a length of 2×4 wrapped in a carpet scrap) across the tiled surface while tapping it lightly with a hammer or rubber mallet.

Also check tiles frequently with a layout stick to make sure they maintain alignment. **4–5.** You can make small corrections by wiggling the tiles until they are true. If a tile sinks below the surface of surrounding tiles, remove it, add more adhesive, and reset it.

Job Site Safety

Tiling is certainly not the most dangerous kind of construction work. But there are several operations where you need to take sensible precautions and protect yourself.

Ventilation. When working with an organic adhesive or other volatile or toxic material, you need to provide ventilation according to the manufacturer's recommendations. Bear this in mind when you are using cleaning materials, too. Check product labels for cautions. You may also need to wear a respirator and safety gloves.

Cutting. Snap cutters are safe tools to use because handle positions are removed from the cutting and splitting action. Nippers are also safe if you use them correctly and take only very small bites. You need to take more care using a wet saw. Although wet-saw blades generally don't have cutting teeth, the coated abrasive edge spins at high speed. The sensible approach is to keep your hands at the sides of the feed table; then be sure that the tile is firmly seated, and feed the tile into the blade gradually.

Tile Tip   Laying Out Floors

Laser levels emit a light beam that shows clearly on almost any surface. The tools are used mainly to establish level points. But they also are handy in tile work, where they can project layout lines.

Battery-powered laser levels *project a beam of light. You can use one to establish level points or to display working guidelines on floors and walls.*

With a laser layout line projected across the floor, you don't have to hold back adhesive to keep from covering the line the way you must with chalk lines.

Installing Field Tiles

Tools and Materials   *Moderate*

- Chalk-line box
- Notched trowel
- Tile spacers
- Tile adhesive

TILE TIP: *Chalk lines can mark the center of the room, and also set up working guidelines if you snap them along grout seams.*

1 *You can plan the layout based only on measurements, but it's wise to set out a few rows on your snapped lines and see how the field fits the room.*

2 *Use a notched trowel to spread the tile adhesive up to your guidelines. Match the notch depth to the adhesive and tile type.*

3 *Set the tiles into the ribbed adhesive bed. You need only moderate pressure to embed them and create a secure bond.*

4 *Set spacers to maintain the grid layout. Some spacers may remain under grout; others must be removed. (Check with the manufacturer.)*

5 *Use your layout stick every few rows or so to check the tile alignment. You can also make sure the grid is square by measuring off the walls.*

Installing Partial Tiles

Tools and Materials   *Moderate*

- Marker or pencil
- Snap tile cutter
- Scoring tool
- Tile nippers
- Notched trowel and tile adhesive

TILE TIP: *On edge cuts you can often save time with the tile nipper (and some broken tiles) by first scoring and cutting off a waste section with a snap cutter.*

1 To mark border tiles, set a full tile on top of the tile at the edge of the field, and another tile on it to find and mark the margin to the wall.

3 On most tiles, you need to draw the scoring wheel across the surface firmly but only once to slice through the glaze and get a clean snap.

4 To break the tile cleanly, most snap cutters have a handle connected to a pressure plate that pushes down evenly on both sides of the score line.

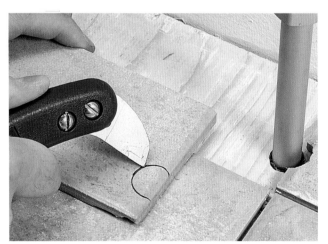

6 On partial tiles that meet an obstruction along the edge of the room, you can use a scoring tool to crack the glaze before cutting with a nipper.

7 Start nipping very small pieces of the cutout section, working gradually up to your cut line. You may want to file cut edges in exposed installations.

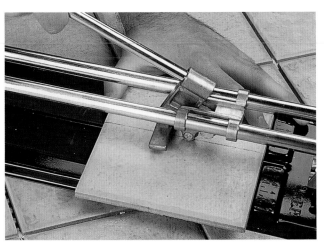

2 Use a snap cutter to score the surface of the tile along your mark. You need to draw the scoring arm toward you with firm pressure.

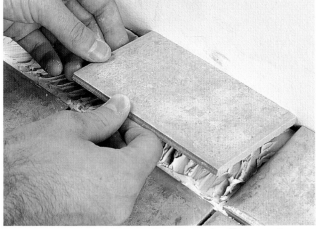

5 Use a notched trowel to spread adhesive along the edge of the tile field. Then set the partial tile in place using spacers if need be.

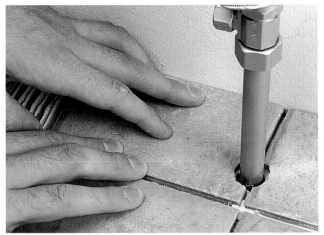

8 Fit the trimmed partial tile into place on a bed of ribbed adhesive. Remember to leave enough space in the cutouts for grout or caulking.

Cutting Partial Tiles

If you start with full tiles in a corner, you can get into trouble when the field reaches the opposite walls. To avoid cutting uneven pieces, you should lay the main field in the center of the room so that you can use partial tiles of the same size around the edges. This approach also makes the job go faster.

In situations where the layout won't allow equal sizes of partial tiles, the best plan is to use full tiles in the most visible portion of the room, and save the small or irregular pieces for a less important or partially concealed border—for example, the wall normally concealed behind an open door.

When all of the full tiles in the main field are down, cut and place all the partial tiles around the room perimeter. If you plan to use cove or trim tiles, you have to allow for the thickness (and a grout joint) against the wall. If the field tiles run to the wall, leave a slight gap between the tiles and wall for expansion.

Offset Measuring. To cut partial field and border tiles, place a loose tile directly on top of the full-size tile next to the space to be filled. Place another loose tile on top of that one, and move it against the wall. Use the back edge of that top tile as a guide, and draw a line on the surface of the loose tile below. That's the one you cut. This offset method of measuring is also handy if you need to trim L-shaped tiles at corners.

A well-planned layout and accurately cut tiles create an appealing living space.

Thresholds

Thresholds (sometimes called saddles) can be wood, metal, or marble strips that bridge gaps between different types of floors. They can also make a transition between floors that are almost but not quite level with each other—for example, where a tiled bath floor is slightly higher than the wood floor in a hallway. You attach the threshold to the underlayment and tile up to it. Most wood and metal saddles are attached with nails or screws. (You can conceal the screwheads in wooden saddles with putty or plugs.) Marble saddles, which are typically used at bathroom doors, are set in a bed of adhesive. Whatever type you use, plan for thresholds during the layout stage.

Wooden Threshold

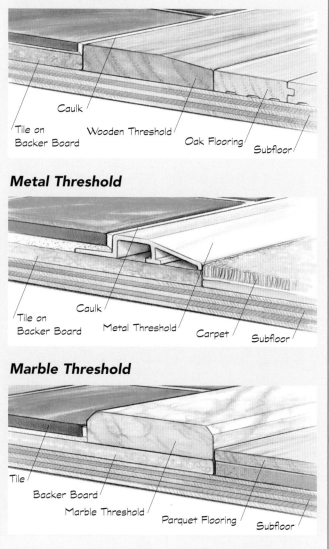

Caulk

Tile on Backer Board   Wooden Threshold   Oak Flooring   Subfloor

Metal Threshold

Caulk

Tile on Backer Board   Metal Threshold   Carpet   Subfloor

Marble Threshold

Tile

Backer Board

Marble Threshold   Parquet Flooring   Subfloor

Applying the Grout

Before you grout the tile joints, the adhesive has to cure. That could take 24 to 48 hours. Check the manufacturer's recommendations to be sure. Then take the time to clean any dirt or debris from the joints, and remove spacers, if necessary.

If you are using tile that is easily stained, you can protect the surface with a removable sealer. Make sure the sealer has cured fully before applying the grout. Generally, ceramic tiles do not become stained from grout—or almost anything else. It's normally the grout itself that becomes stained.

Mix the grout according to manufacturer's instructions. **1.** Plan on mixing enough to fill all the seams. Even over a large area, grout goes down quickly. Most people have success using a rubber float to spread grout, but you can also try a squeegee. Plunk down a trowel full of the material, and start working it into the joints by sweeping your float at a diagonal to the field pattern. You need to sweep the float back and forth, pushing the pile of grout, making several passes over the same area to compact the grout into the joints. **2.**

Do not use grout to fill the joint between the last row of floor tiles and the wall. Instead, use flexible silicone caulk to allow for expansion and contraction between the different materials.

As soon as the grout becomes firm, use a wet sponge to wipe off excess grout from the tile surface. **3–4.** You might use a squeegee to clear any streaks of grout material; then start with the sponge. On most jobs it takes several passes (rinsing the sponge frequently and changing the water, too) before the final grout haze is cleaned up.

Tooling & Sealing Joints

You may be able to leave the grout joints flush, or nearly flush, just by working the seams with your trowel. Another option is to tool, or strike, the joints to create slightly recessed seams. (You can also do this before cleaning the excess.) Many common objects can do the job, including a toothbrush handle, small spoon, or a shaped stick.

Clean off the tiles again, and smooth the joints using a damp sponge. This will leave yet another haze that you can polish away with a clean, damp cloth. In most cases, the grout will take several days to cure completely. You may need to wait longer before applying a sealer; check the grout label directions.

In wet areas (mainly bathrooms) you can retard surface mold and protect grout seams by adding a sealer, such as liquid silicone. **5.** Start in the corner farthest away from the door, and apply a thin, even coat of sealer on the grout only. Some sealers come with a built-in applicator, or you can use an artist's brush.

Grouting and Sealing

Tools and Materials   Easy

- Bucket and sponges
- Rags
- Float
- Grout mix
- Grout bag (optional)

TILE TIP: *To wipe off the grout haze, use several large sponges, rinsing in clean water after every few passes. Without regular rinsing, you'll just respread the haze.*

1 *On most jobs, the best approach is to mix only the grout you need. You can buy color-matched grout or add powdered colorant to the mix.*

2 *Use a float (or a squeegee) to push the grout into the seams. Make sweeping strokes at a diagonal to the grid pattern of the tile field.*

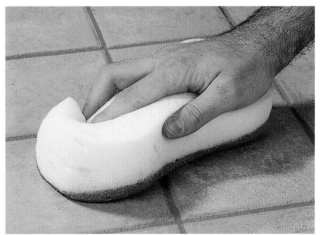

3 *When the grout sets up (you may want to strike off the seams first), start to clean up the remaining surface glaze with a clean, damp sponge.*

4 *Even after several passes with a sponge, you may need to remove a final haze by polishing the tile surface with a clean, damp cloth.*

5 *In wet areas such as kitchens and baths, consider one more step: sealing the grout seams (generally with a liquid silicone) to reduce maintenance.*

Installing Slate Tile

It's hard to beat slate for an entryway or foyer floor. It's attractive, durable, slip resistant, and nearly waterproof when properly installed. Dirty shoes, boots, and sneakers don't stain the surface, and their mess can be cleaned quickly with a damp mop.

Slate manufacturers have developed uniform ¼-inch-thick tiles that can de installed over cementitious backer board using heavy duty mastic. These tiles come in a wide range of colors from grays and blues to reds and browns. And they're sometimes sold in packages that have a variety of precut sizes, from 6 × 6-inch units up to 12 × 24-inch pieces. Slate is more often found in simple 12 × 12-inch squares, which is what we used here.

Preparing the Floor

If the current floor is wood flooring, you will have to remove it to get down to the subflooring. If it's vinyl or carpet, you'll have to remove the finish material and the underlayment beneath it to get to the subfloor. In all cases, be sure to carefully remove the baseboard molding surrounding the area so that it can be used again. Once the subfloor is exposed, renail any loose or squeaky sections using 8d common nails driven through the subfloor and into the floor joists below.

In most cases, the top of your new slate floor will be higher than the finished surface was before. Because of this you will have to cut all the door casings that abut the floor area so that the tiles can fit underneath. The same could be true of any interior door that swings over

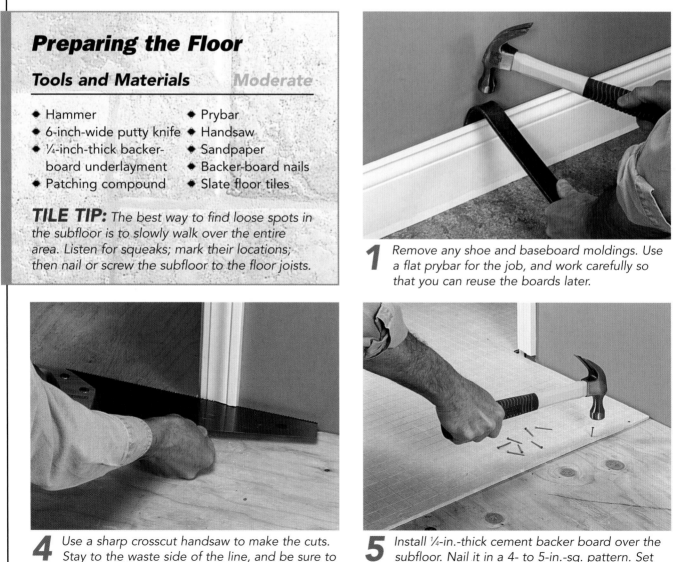

Preparing the Floor

Tools and Materials   *Moderate*

- Hammer
- 6-inch-wide putty knife
- ¼-inch-thick backer-board underlayment
- Patching compound
- Prybar
- Handsaw
- Sandpaper
- Backer-board nails
- Slate floor tiles

TILE TIP: *The best way to find loose spots in the subfloor is to slowly walk over the entire area. Listen for squeaks; mark their locations; then nail or screw the subfloor to the floor joists.*

1 Remove any shoe and baseboard moldings. Use a flat prybar for the job, and work carefully so that you can reuse the boards later.

4 Use a sharp crosscut handsaw to make the cuts. Stay to the waste side of the line, and be sure to stop before cutting the doorjamb board.

5 Install ¼-in.-thick cement backer board over the subfloor. Nail it in a 4- to 5-in.-sq. pattern. Set the heads below the board surface.

the new floor. If it was close to rubbing the floor before, it almost certainly will after the slate is installed. Don't worry about your entry door. These doors always swing over thresholds, which provide plenty of clearance.

Install Underlayment

Vacuum the surface clean; then start installing the backer-board panels. These ¼-in.-thick sheets come in 4 × 8-foot panels and are easy to carry and to cut. Plan the seams between sheets so that they don't fall over seams in the subfloor below. It is important that the backer board be nailed securely to the subfloor. Use underlayment nails and drive them in a 4 to 5-inch-square grid over the entire surface.

Set all the nailheads just below the surface with a nail

set. Then cover the nailheads and fill any cracks between panels with floor-patching compound. Once this dries, sand the surface smooth using 100-grit sandpaper, and vacuum up the dust.

Laying Out the Tile

Check the product packaging of your tile to see if it recommends a pattern. If it does not, create a layout that looks good and minimizes cutting. Also check for color on the individual tiles. If one tile is particularly eye-catching, try to use it in an obvious location. Tiles that aren't as attractive can be used near the walls. Once you're satisfied with your arrangement, put a piece of masking tape on each tile, and mark it with a number so that you will be sure that it is installed in the right place.

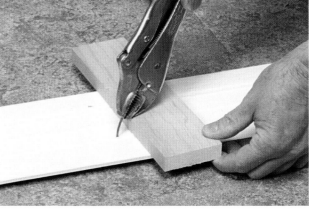

2 Once a molding board is pried from the wall, pull the nails out from the backside using locking pliers and a scrap block for leverage.

3 Door casings may need to be trimmed before installation. Place a tile on a piece of backer board, and scribe a line on the casing.

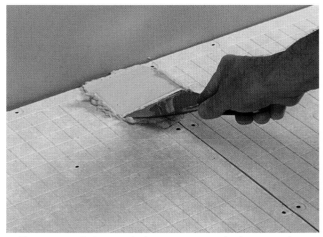

6 Once all the underlayment is nailed, cover the nail heads and any seams in the backer-board panels with floor-patching compound.

7 Place the tiles on the dry underlayment to achieve the best looking layout. Try to minimize cutting by adjusting the layout as necessary.

Laying Slate Tile

Once you are satisfied with your tile layout, make any necessary cuts using a circular saw with an abrasive or masonry blade. Cutting the material is pretty easy; the saw has more than enough power for the job. But the cutting generates a tremendous amount of dust and noise. Be sure to wear safety glasses, ear protection, and a dust mask. And if possible, make the cuts outside.

Begin spreading the mastic in the least accessible corner. To get the best coverage, use a sweeping motion, and hold the trowel at a 45-degree angle. Cover a 2 to 3-foot section; then start laying the tiles in place. Carefully set each in the mastic, twisting them back and forth a little to set them securely. Insert spacers between the tiles to keep uniform grout lines. We used ¼-inch-thick plastic spacers. Continue working away from the corner, alternating between spreading the mastic and laying the tile in easily managed sections. Remove the spacers from each section before you move onto the next. Let the mastic dry for 24 hours without walking on the tiles.

Grouting

Latex grout is generally recommended for slate floors. The grout comes dry, and you mix it with water until it has the consistency of wet sand. Once you're satisfied with the mix, begin working the grout into the spaces between the tiles. A flat pointing trowel is a good tool to use, especially to finish the surface of the grout. But using it is slow. Faster methods, such as applying the

Installing the Slate

Tools and Materials   Moderate

- ◆ Circular saw with abrasive blade
- ◆ Paint brush
- ◆ Wood or plastic grout spacers
- ◆ Notched trowel
- ◆ Flat pointing trowel
- ◆ Mastic, grout sealer
- ◆ Sponge
- ◆ Burlap rag, sawdust

TILE TIP: *Creating a dry layout before installing the slate leads to a more attractive project, as you can place less attractive tiles in less visible locations.*

1 *Slate is easy to cut using a standard circular saw with an abrasive or masonry blade. Wear eye, ear, and breathing protection when cutting.*

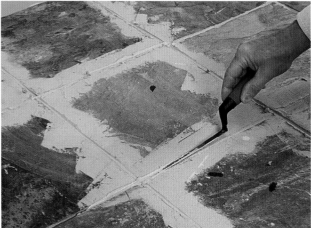

4 *Let the mastic dry according to the manufacturer's specifications. Then mix the grout, and spread it into the spaces between the tiles.*

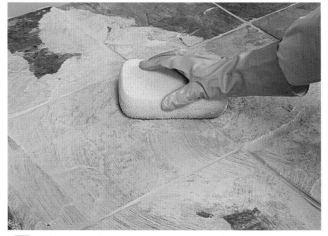

5 *Clean up the grout as you go using a sponge and clean water. It's much easier to remove the grout now while it's still damp.*

grout with a rubber trowel, tend to be sloppier, and the time you save getting the grout into the cracks will probably be used up in extra cleaning time. Be sure to fill each joint completely, and clean up the tile surfaces as you go. Clean water and a sponge that's rinsed frequently do a good job. If the grout is allowed to dry completely on the surface of the tile, it's very difficult to remove.

When the grout is dry to the touch, spread some sawdust on the floor, and rub it over the surface with a clean burlap cloth. This should remove any grout haze that may still be on the surface of the tiles. Be careful not to dislodge the grout. When you're done with this step, vacuum up all the dust, and let the grout joints cure for three days before walking on them.

Sealing

While it's not necessary to seal a slate floor, many people feel that coating it prevents the grout from staining over time. If you want to seal your floor, wait a full month after the installation; then clean the floor thoroughly with a damp sponge. Apply the sealer in a thin, uniform first coat using a paintbrush. Most sealers of this type dry in a couple of hours and can be recoated at that time. But be sure to follow the directions of the product you buy. Two coats should do the trick for most floors. Just stay off the floor for 24 hours after the second coat to avoid leaving footprints behind. Reinstall the shoe and baseboard moldings that you removed at the beginning of the project. Finish up the job by touching up any damaged paint.

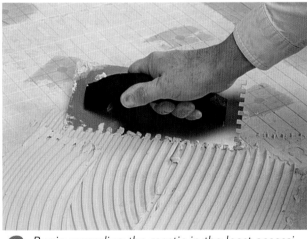

2 Begin spreading the mastic in the least accessible corner, and work out, holding the notched trowel at a 45-deg. angle.

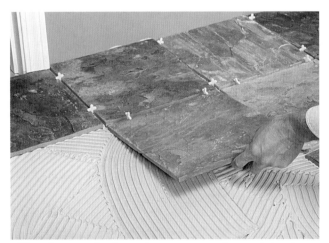

3 Place each tile in the mastic, and twist it back and forth to set it properly. Use plastic spacers to keep the grout lines consistent.

6 Once the grout is dry, clean and polish the slate by sprinkling the surface with sawdust and rubbing it with a burlap rag.

7 Sealing the floor will keep the grout clean and the slate shiny. But you should wait about a month after the tile installation is complete.

DESIGN IDEAS: FLOORS

Stone tiles, left, are a good choice for mudrooms and entries.

Mosaic tiles, above, add texture to a bathroom floor.

Traditional designs, below left, are possible with mosaic tiles.

Kitchen floors, below right, were made for ceramic and stone tiles.

Natural stone, opposite, sets the stage for a dramatic inset design.

DESIGN IDEAS: FLOORS

Tile inset, above left, creates a dramatic entry.

Marble, left, adds an elegant touch.

Hexagon tiles, above, provide a transition to outside.

Terra-cotta tiles, opposite, work well in mudrooms.

CHAPTER 4

TILING WALLS

More than any other surface, perhaps, walls provide an opportunity to combine decoration and durability. In fact, you may find more choices in wall tiles than in any other kind.

At the other end of the spectrum, a wall can serve as a blank canvas for unique, hand-painted tile murals or bold designs of contrasting colors and shapes. Most tile is available with edging components to trim partial installations.

Because tiles resist heat, water, and a variety of stains, they are well suited to kitchen and bathroom walls where easy maintenance is a prime concern. In kitchens, of course, tiles often bridge the gap between countertops and upper cabinets. You also find tile used on walls behind sinks and stoves.

In bathrooms, tile is often used to line shower stalls and tub surrounds. But you can give a bathroom a more open, unified feeling by extending the tile to adjacent walls. Behind a vanity, you can extend a tile backsplash up the wall to frame a mirror. And wall tiles with trim strips can frame windows, doors, and other architectural features in any room of the house.

Design & Layout

The same basic design considerations that apply to floors—color, size, shape, texture, and pattern—also apply to walls. However, when planning your layout, bear in mind that most wall applications incorporate a design that uses tiles of contrasting colors. This makes estimating the number of tiles a bit more difficult and requires a more precise layout.

Tile work on walls often involves different types and shapes of trim pieces, such as tiles with a bullnose edge. You may also need to use special shapes to handle inside and outside corners. These special shapes can make a tile job look very elegant, but they complicate the layout. You need to account for the grout joints, of course, but also for the odd-size portion of the trim piece that turns an inside or outside corner.

If you plan to tile both the walls and the floor, you have two sets of layouts to deal with. Each one may require an adjustment to make a balanced installation. But you need to concentrate on the area along the floor where the two systems meet. You should align grout seams there, if at all possible.

One approach is to start these projects by installing the row of cove or other finishing tiles at the floor level. Coves make a very low-maintenance detail (a great help in kitchens and baths) because the rounded cove base eliminates hard-edged, dirt-trapping corners.

Because this row makes the transition between floor and wall, it's important to have full tiles on both sides if possible. That means you can't adjust the main tile field of the floor on one side, or the wall on the other, which could leave small, partial tiles at the opposite wall or the ceiling. The best bet is to lay out tiles with spacers for grout joints (or make an accurate layout stick) and see where the field tiles will fall.

Once you have positioned the cove tiles, you can work your way up the wall. Save the floor for last so that you don't damage or blemish the new tile with adhesive or grout as you work on the wall.

Patterns & Unique Designs

Many tile manufacturers now make integrated tile systems. For example, in addition to field tiles they offer rectangular pieces for borders, half-rounded accent strips, caps, and several other shapes all designed to work in the same basic grid. With these systems it is relatively easy to plan out a repeating wall scheme. And the grout seams will align.

If you are creating your own design, the amount of detail you can include is determined in part by three elements: the size of the wall, the size of the design, and

Design Options

No design is bad if it's in your own house and represents the style you like. Colors and patterns are matters of personal taste, after all. But before you undertake a tile project covering most or all of a wall, it pays to experiment.

You can do this on a piece of graph paper, using colored pencils to sketch in your ideas at a realistic scale. And you can rummage through tile supply houses trying different combinations. But also consider design services that are increasingly available to do-it-yourselfers.

If you have a home computer, you may be able to use home-design software to create tile patterns complete with bath fixtures, lights, and a mirror.

Now some home-center chains and design-build contracting firms also offer computer-aided design (CAD) services. They allow you to plan a layout for a specific wall area and try different combinations of tile. The most sophisticated software creates three-dimensional views showing how the finished project might look, although they may dress up the view with stock furniture and other fixtures.

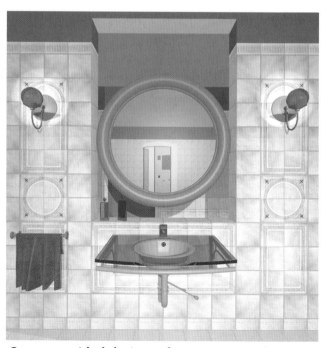

Computer-aided design *software programs let you experiment with different tile patterns and colors on your home computer screen.*

the size of the tiles. Bear in mind that geometric patterns are the easiest to create and install because the basic building blocks are geometric units. It's more difficult to create and install a free-flowing pattern. For example, if you want to create a curved design along a set of stairs, you will have to make many precise cuts.

Cutting Tiles

A good layout plan will help determine in advance where you need cut tiles. The trick is arranging the main field so that you do not end up with a narrow row in a conspicuous place.

Cut tiles should be more than half a tile wide. Ideally, they should be equal widths at opposite sides of a room, to provide symmetry. Sometimes you can adjust the edge sizes by adjusting the width of all the grout joints.

Also be aware of where cut tiles may be needed around doorways, windows, cabinets, and countertops, and whether it would look better to plan the layout so that partial tiles are moved away from these focal points. For example, cut tiles on either side of a window or door opening should be the same width for the opening to appear centered. In the same way, if you are tiling around a fireplace, the wall installation will probably look best if you use full tiles on the sides and save partial tiles or irregular pieces for the corners of the room.

One approach is to plan the main field, and then see where you can add a repeating pattern of accent tiles.

With computer design programs, you can create a rough view of an area using stock versions of rugs and other fixtures to build your "before" picture.

Define the area you want to change, the floor in this case, and insert different shapes and patterns that change carpeting into tile.

Planning for Materials

To estimate the amount of tiles you need, disregard small obstructions when you're measuring square footage. Subtract only for a large window, built-in sink, or cabinet. It's wise to figure about 5 to 10 percent for waste. If your installation includes different-color tiles, use your drawing to count the actual number of tiles of each color, adding the same percentage for miscuts and breakage. If the layout includes cut tiles, count each partial tile as a full tile.

If you are extending tile to adjoining walls or across a doorway, you will want to align the horizontal grout joints. It's often best to use full tiles where walls join, but you should check how the field tiles will fall when they reach the edges of the project area. If you center full tiles over a doorway, for example, you might end up with cut tiles of two different widths at opposite ends of the wall. You can't very well reshape your rooms to match a tile grid. But if you check several possible layouts, you can generally find one that has full tiles where you notice the pattern and partial tiles where you don't.

If you're working with mural tiles (or almost any distinct pattern within the main tile field), you may need to account for a large block of tiles. Most murals come in sets of tiles—from as few as four to well over 50—with each tile representing a piece of the picture. Plan these installations by taking the overall dimensions of the mural and adjusting the set of tiles on the wall. You may be able to balance the layout on a wall and avoid small pieces at the corners by using border tiles.

Basic Tile Combinations

You can use different sizes, shapes, and colors to create a nearly limitless number of tile patterns and combinations. But even if you stick to one size, there are three basic ways to set them on the wall.

Jack-on-Jack. This is the easiest way to lay wall tiles, aligning the grout joints and stacking one tile directly on top of another.

Running Bond. This is the same kind of pattern used on most brick walls, with the joints of one course centered under full tiles in the next row.

Diagonal Jack-on-Jack. This is the basic system of aligned joints turned sideways 45 degrees, which makes square tiles look diamond-shaped. The drawback is that every tile in the rows at the floor and ceiling have to be trimmed.

Jack-on-jack layouts have tiles stacked directly on top of each other in columns. With this system, all the grout joints between tiles are aligned.

Running bond layouts have the joints in one course offset to fall over the center of tiles below. The offset is accentuated with contrasting colors.

Diagonal jack-on-jack layouts have the basic stacked tile pattern turned sideways on the wall. This gives square tiles a diamond-shaped appearance.

Preparing Walls for Tile

Most interior walls are surfaced with gypsum wallboard. In many older homes the walls are plastered. Both materials generally make a good backing for ceramic tile if the surface is sound, flat, and smooth. You also can tile over sound wood or masonry walls. It's not a good idea to tile over wallpaper, fabric, or any other surface that is not strong enough by itself to support tile.

In new construction, of course, a taped and finished drywall surface will make an ideal base for tile. But in existing rooms you may have to make some repairs and improvements to be sure that the tile job will last. There are two basic options: bury surface problems under a new layer of drywall, or fix the existing wall.

In addition to the surface repairs, you may want to make some changes that are more than skin deep, such as relocating an electrical outlet or moving an in-wall air conditioner. If there are problems with the wall framing, you should strip off the old surface, fix the problems, and install new drywall. Remember that tile needs exceptionally firm support to keep grout joints from cracking. If there is movement in the wall—for instance, due to a water leak—the tile job isn't likely to last.

Wall Strength

Generally, a wall is considered too weak for tile if you can flex the surface by pressing the heel of your hand against a panel midway between two studs. Adding another layer of drywall should do the trick, but even

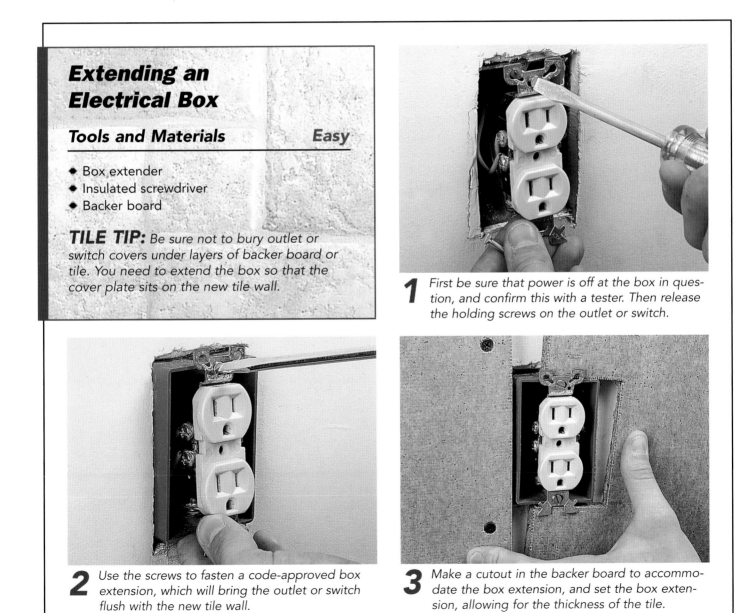

Extending an Electrical Box

Tools and Materials   Easy

- Box extender
- Insulated screwdriver
- Backer board

TILE TIP: Be sure not to bury outlet or switch covers under layers of backer board or tile. You need to extend the box so that the cover plate sits on the new tile wall.

1 First be sure that power is off at the box in question, and confirm this with a tester. Then release the holding screws on the outlet or switch.

2 Use the screws to fasten a code-approved box extension, which will bring the outlet or switch flush with the new tile wall.

3 Make a cutout in the backer board to accommodate the box extension, and set the box extension, allowing for the thickness of the tile.

½ inch of extra wall thickness can pose problems around window and door trim.

You can refasten loose panels with drywall screws spaced 8 to 10 inches apart along all framing members. You can locate studs and other framing behind the wall with an inexpensive magnetic stud finder.

If the panels are too thin or weak to support the tile, a second layer of ½-inch wallboard or cement backer board over the existing panels will provide extra rigidity. When covering existing panels with new ones, make sure that the joints between the new panels do not fall directly over those in the existing wall.

If necessary, you can reinforce wall framing with blocking or additional studs. In general, studs should have a maximum spacing of 16 inches on center, and wallboard or other backing materials should be a minimum of ½ inch thick.

Existing Wall Surfaces

On walls covered with paneling or wallpaper, you'll need to strip the old surface. Paneling is easy enough to remove; you just pull the trim and pry off the sheets. Removing wallpaper can be trickier.

You can roll on a liquid wallpaper remover or rent a steamer box to loosen the paper adhesive. These systems generally work better if you first scuff up the paper surface with a scarifying tool. When you scrape away the residue, try not to dig into the drywall surface.

Even if the wallboard or plaster is sound, you should not set tile if the surface paint is loose or peeling. Prepare these surfaces basically the same way you would for repainting. Start by scraping away any loose paint. Then fill deep gouges with joint compound, and rough up any remaining glossy surfaces with sandpaper.

Walls in Wet Areas

If you are tiling a wall that is subject to moisture or water—for example, behind a kitchen sink or in a bathroom or laundry room—you need to install some type of waterproofing membrane, water-resistant backing, or both. The most common application is a layer of cement-based backer board attached with corrosion-resistant nails or screws.

Depending on the extent of moisture exposure, a waterproof membrane also may be required. This is an important step that many do-it-yourselfers make the mistake of omitting. There are several types, including liquid membranes and the old standby, 15-pound roofing felt. The most common (and the one recommended for backer board) is 4-mil polyethylene sheets. You may want to check local building codes for recommended waterproofing materials.

Wall tiles in wet areas *around baths and sinks should be supported by panels of cement-based backer board.*

Removing Base Trim

Tools and Materials   Moderate

- Pry bar
- Screwdriver
- Hammer
- Masking tape and marker
- Wooden shims

TILE TIP: Trim in an older home can be very brittle and easy to break. If you plan to reinstall it, pry gently, gradually working your way along the boards.

1 Once you get a piece of trim loose with a hammer and screwdriver, use gradual pressure with a pry bar to move it away from the wall.

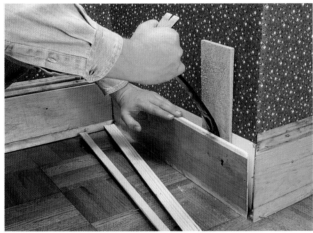

2 To remove large pieces of baseboard trim without damaging the wall, insert a wooden shim behind the board when you pry.

3 On long boards, you may need to use several screwdrivers, chisels, or similar tools as wedges while you work the piece free.

4 To remove stubborn nails, set a bar between the nail points and the wall, and tap on the baseboard to expose the heads so that you can pull them.

5 Label the location of each piece as you remove it. On a room with many corners, this will make it easier to reinstall the trim.

Patching Drywall

The good news is that you don't have to patch every minor dent and scratch, because they will be filled by the tile adhesive. But you should repair holes and fix popped nails, bubbled joint tape, and other problems that could keep the tile from sitting flat on the wall.

Instead of driving loose nails back into drywall, pull them and drive a drywall screw near the old hole. Along joints, check for splits or bubbles in the drywall tape. If you find raised or loose sections, slice the damaged tape from the wall using a utility knife, and replace it with fiberglass mesh tape embedded in the tile adhesive.

There are several ways to repair larger cracks and holes. The most drastic is to cut out a section of the damaged drywall running from one stud to another,

although this entails so much cutting that you might as well replace the entire sheet. In most cases, you can add mesh to reinforce a patch or cut out the damaged area and add a patch piece of solid drywall.

Over small holes—for example, where you have some crumbling around holes for plumbing pipes—you can use self-stick fiberglass mesh to bridge the gaps and reinforce a filling layer of joint compound. For doorknob-sized holes, you can use a mesh patch kit that comes with an extra reinforcing panel.

One good way to fix large holes is to cut a clean-edged rectangular opening around the damage, and reinforce the edges with short lengths of 1x3 fastened to the inside face of the drywall. The exposed edges of the wood strips can support a solid drywall patch.

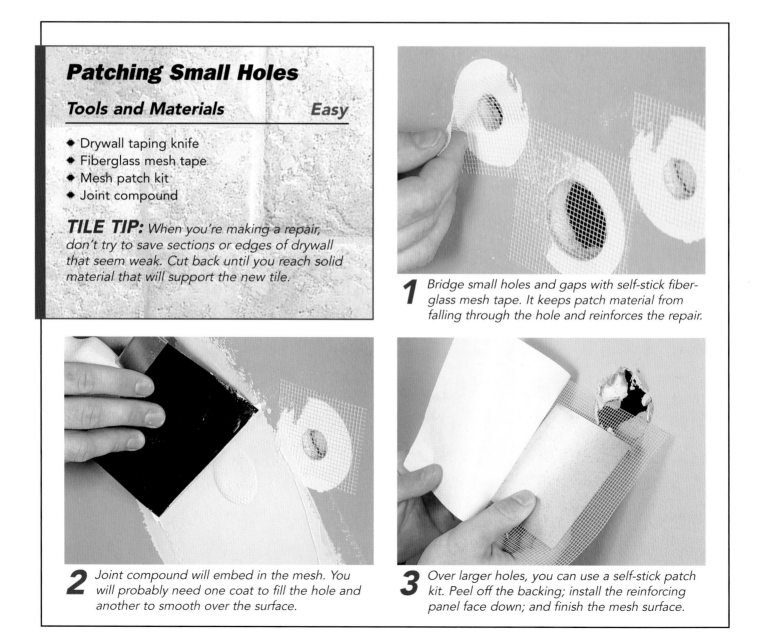

Patching Small Holes

Tools and Materials   Easy

- Drywall taping knife
- Fiberglass mesh tape
- Mesh patch kit
- Joint compound

TILE TIP: When you're making a repair, don't try to save sections or edges of drywall that seem weak. Cut back until you reach solid material that will support the new tile.

1 Bridge small holes and gaps with self-stick fiberglass mesh tape. It keeps patch material from falling through the hole and reinforces the repair.

2 Joint compound will embed in the mesh. You will probably need one coat to fill the hole and another to smooth over the surface.

3 Over larger holes, you can use a self-stick patch kit. Peel off the backing; install the reinforcing panel face down; and finish the mesh surface.

Patching Large Holes

Tools and Materials   Easy

- Drywall saw or utility knife
- Caulking gun and adhesive
- Drill and drywall screws
- Drywall taping knife
- Tape and joint compound
- Sandpaper, sanding pad, or sanding mesh

TILE TIP: *Use dry furring strips or other wood strips to avoid shrinking that could disrupt the patch repair and the tiles above.*

1 Cut out the damaged area, leaving a clean-edged rectangle. Then cut 1x3 furring strips; hold them to the drywall; and fasten with screws.

2 Apply construction adhesive to the exposed half of the side braces. You can also add adhesive to the furring strips before you install them.

3 Set the patch piece of drywall on the braces, move it back and forth to set in the adhesive, and secure it with drywall screws.

4 Make sure that the screwheads are flush, and cover the seams with paper or fiberglass tape embedded with joint compound.

5 With tile, you don't need to make a perfect repair, but you may want to add one extra coat, and sand away rough edges of compound.

Preparing & Repairing Plaster

Extensive cracking in a plaster wall often indicates regular seasonal movement in the building, which can disrupt tile. In severe cases, you may need to strip the surface, although a layer of glued-and-screwed cement backer board may work. If the plaster is soft and cracks or crumbles when you poke it with a screwdriver, it should be removed.

Fill small holes or depressions with patching plaster. Clean and moisten the area, and spread the fresh plaster with a wide drywall taping knife. When the patch dries, fill it to the surface, let it dry, and sand it flush.

If the plaster is sound, wash it thoroughly with a general-purpose cleaner to remove dirt or grease. Sand a glossy painted surface to ensure a good adhesive bond.

Repairing Outside Corners

Corners that project into a room (around pass-through openings, for example) often take the most abuse and show the most damage—both in drywall and plaster walls. If the damage is minor, you can usually repair it with drywall joint compound and a wide drywall knife. Use a straightedge to shape the corner edge, or smooth out one side and let it dry before you work on the adjoining surface.

If the damage is extensive, you may need to cut away the corner reinforcement. Although some corners may have only paper-taped edges that are easy to remove, most have metal corner guards secured with nails. Once the guard is damaged, you may have to pull the nails and remove it (or a piece of it) and install new edging.

Patching Plaster

Tools and Materials   *Easy*

- Wide drywall taping knife
- Patching plaster
- Primer and roller or brush
- Masonry trowel

TILE TIP: *It's wise to seal large areas of fresh plaster or joint compound so that the dry material does not pull excessive moisture from the tile adhesive and weaken the tile bond.*

1 Use patching plaster to fill the damaged area in layers. Score the undercoat surface. When dry, moisten before troweling on the finish coat.

2 Use a wide blade to smooth out the finish coat. Let one edge ride on the adjacent wall to keep the patch flush. Sand down any ridges.

3 When the finish coat is dry, prime the patch to keep the dry, unsealed material from drawing moisture from the tile adhesive.

Fixing a Corner

Tools and Materials   Moderate

* Utility knife
* Hacksaw
* Metal snips
* Corner guard
* Drill and screws
* Putty knife and joint compound

TILE TIP: *If the corner guard has a dent in it but is still secure, try filling the area with joint compound. Always replace a loose guard.*

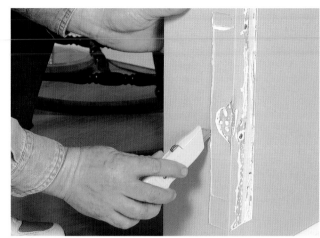

1 To get at a damaged section of corner guard, you may have to cut through layers of paint and joint compound with a utility knife.

2 Once the guard is exposed, use a hacksaw to cut through the metal above and below the damaged section. Pull the nails, and remove it.

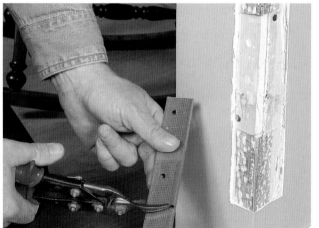

3 Use metal snips to cut a replacement length of guard. Clear away loose drywall paper and compound on the corner before you fasten the piece.

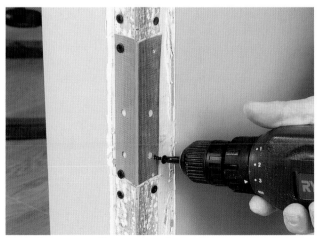

4 Use drywall screws to fasten the replacement guard on the corner. Make sure that the raised corner rib aligns with the original guard.

5 Provide a flat surface for the tile by filling in both sides of the raised corner rib with joint compound. Sand off any raised ridges.

Installing New Drywall

Here are a few of the key steps involved in installing drywall, and some tips on making the job solid enough to support tile securely.

■ *Installation Efficiency.* Most do-it-yourselfers use 4 × 8 sheets standing on end. It's a nice match for standard 8-foot ceiling height, but you can also install sheets horizontally, creating one tape seam down the middle of the wall.

■ *Cutting Holes.* The tool of choice for pros is a pint-sized router with a long straight bit. It can plunge through drywall and closely follow the irregular outline of an electrical box. **1–3.** Most DIY-ers have an easier time controlling a straight-handled utility saw made to cut drywall. Its sharp tip allows you to poke through drywall and start a cut. You can also use a utility knife, but it's difficult (and more dangerous) to use a knife to carve through interior cuts, where a saw offers more control.

■ *Long Cuts.* Even many pros use a 4-foot-long metal T-square to guide a utility knife in a full-width cut through a sheet. Along the 8-foot length of a panel you can snap a chalk guideline. You don't need to press hard on the knife to make the scoring cut. It's more important to slice a straight line than to dig deeply, even if you have to go over your cut again. Then you can snap the panel along the score line, and trim through the remaining paper. **4–5.**

■ *Lifters.* Whether you install sheets vertically or horizontally, the edge resting on the floor has to be raised a bit before you nail. In many houses, the bottom edge will be covered by baseboard trim, while the top edge will form a visible taped and finished joint. Make this job easier by using a panel lifter—a wedge-shaped tool that seesaws over a built-in wheel. **6.** Kick the lifter under the edge of the sheet, and step down on one end; the other end lifts the panel into position quite easily, leaving your hands free.

■ *Nails and Screws.* Do-it-yourselfers normally use nails and a hammer to hang gypsum drywall. Most pros favor screws and a power screwdriver because it's faster and easier, and the screwheads leave small dimples that are easy to finish. **7.** You may want to use a nail or two to hold the sheet in place at first. Then you can step back, load up the drill, and fasten the rest of the sheet with screws.

■ *Taping.* You should be able to get by with only one coat of compound on field fasteners and taped seams. **8.** Don't leave any large ridges that could prevent tiles from seating against the wall.

Installing Drywall

Tools and Materials   *Moderate*

- ◆ Measuring tape and marker
- ◆ Utility knife and saw
- ◆ Panel lifter
- ◆ Drill with a screwdriver bit and screws
- ◆ Taping supplies

TILE TIP: *You can use special-order ¼-in.-thick drywall sheets to resurface walls. But they are so whippy and easy to break that it's better to use ⅜-in. panels.*

3 Use the sharp tip of a utility saw to poke through the panel at the corners of the box. Then you can cut along the marks with the saw teeth.

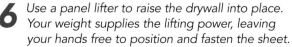

6 Use a panel lifter to raise the drywall into place. Your weight supplies the lifting power, leaving your hands free to position and fasten the sheet.

1 It's easy enough to measure the overall width you need. But you have to measure very carefully to locate an outlet or switch in the panel section.

2 Locate the sides of the box and measure up from the bottom of the sheet to find its height. Always double-check measurements before cutting.

4 To trim the drywall panel to overall size, mark or snap a cutting guideline and score along the mark with a sharp utility knife.

5 Slide the panel waste section beyond its supports, and snap down to crack the gypsum in a straight line. Then slice through the backing paper.

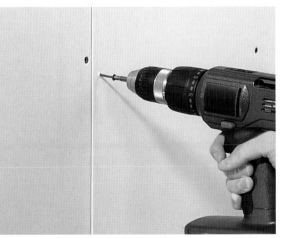

7 Use a variable-speed drill to drive wide-threaded wallboard screws. They provide more holding power and are less likely to pop out than nails.

8 To prepare new drywall for tile, a one- or two-coat taping job should do. Fill feathered panel edges so that the tile will be evenly supported.

Installing Wall Tile

Installing wall tile follows the same general procedures as installing floor tile. But you lay wall tiles from the lowest point up so that the tiles and spacers can support the next course. Most adhesives used for wall tile are formulated to hold the tiles in place while still wet. These include thinset latex-portland cement and organic mastic adhesives.

Establishing Working Lines

On simple wall installations, you can establish a vertical working line near the base of the wall and a horizontal line at or near the center point of the wall. Then you start laying tiles at the intersection of the two lines.

Additional layout lines are helpful if the wall is large or contains openings, counters, cabinets, or other built-in fixtures. It is also a good idea to add lines that locate trim and border tiles. Carefully measured guidelines help you position field tiles in a balanced layout and keep joints aligned as the job progresses.

In most cases, you establish a vertical working line at or near the center of the wall. If the wall has a large window or other opening, you may want to adjust the vertical line so that the opening is centered and tiles on both sides of the opening are the same width.

To establish the vertical line, measure the width of the tiled area, and mark the center point. Use your layout stick (or a row of spaced tiles on the floor) to mark off tile and grout joints on either side of this point.

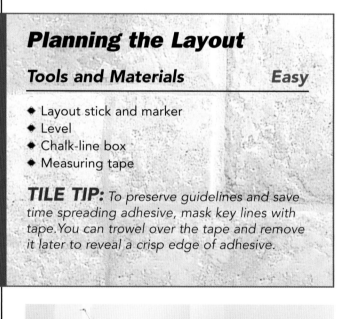

Planning the Layout

Tools and Materials   **Easy**

- Layout stick and marker
- Level
- Chalk-line box
- Measuring tape

TILE TIP: To preserve guidelines and save time spreading adhesive, mask key lines with tape. You can trowel over the tape and remove it later to reveal a crisp edge of adhesive.

1 Starting in the center of the tile area, use your layout stick to transfer a set of carefully measured tile and grout marks to the wall.

4 To leave a clear chalk residue as you snap a line, temporarily pin the line with your finger at midspan, and snap one side and then the other.

5 Use your level to establish a vertical guideline. It's convenient to snap chalk lines on a layout stick tick mark, so you can follow it exactly with tiles.

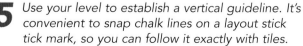

If the last tile at each end is going to be more than half a tile wide, you can use the center point to establish the vertical guideline. If the end tiles are going to be less than half a tile wide, move the vertical guideline a distance of half a tile to the right or left of the centerline. This will result in wider partial tiles at each end.

You also need to establish a level horizontal baseline to ensure that the first row—and all rows above it—will be level. If the wall includes a countertop, vanity, or tub and you are tiling the wall from floor level, you may have to adjust the baseline at the floor. (See page 103, **1.**) Usually, it looks best to have full tiles above these features even if it means having a row of cut tiles at floor level. If you are tiling only partway up the wall, establish another horizontal guide to indicate the limit line.

A Tiling Sequence

There are two basic ways to lay field tile on a wall. You can build up the tiles from the center of the wall in a pyramid shape, or lay the length of the bottom row and work from one corner. Remember that most layouts look best with the full field tiles centered and equal partial tiles at the edges.

If you use trim tiles at floor level, you typically set all of them first and then fill in above them with field tiles. Trim pieces for inside and outside corners are installed just ahead of the whole field tiles, and cut pieces are filled in as needed.

In all cases, you will be building the tile up from the bottom, including grout joint spacers. Each new course is supported by the course beneath it. (See page 103, **2.**).

2 At the edges of the layout area, use a full tile to determine what the margin will be on the cut-tile edges. About half a tile is an ideal margin.

3 Once the vertical layout is settled, use a level to establish a horizontal line. To extend level marks on a large wall, set the level on a straight 2x4.

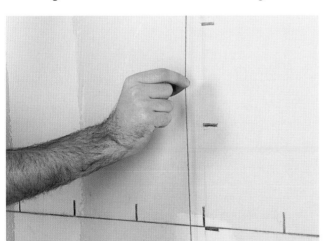

6 Complete your guides with another snapped chalk line. You may want other guides to indicate rows of trim and areas around obstructions.

7 Mark the location of built-in nailers for grab bars or other wall fittings on the floor. Marks on the wall will be obscured by adhesive and then tile.

Cutting Tiles

Use a snap tile cutter to make straight cuts, and a pair of nippers, if necessary, to notch around irregular shapes. If the tiles you're using have ridges on the back, it may help to cut in the same direction that the ridges run. If you want to make a clean hole in the tile to fit around a pipe or other wall fitting, use a carbide-tipped hole saw.

Applying Adhesive

Apply just enough adhesive for you to cover with tile before it skins over or sets up. That area depends on how fast you work, of course, and on the open time of the adhesive. On large walls, start with small sections of about 4 × 4 feet, and spread more adhesive once you get a sense of the working time. **3.**

Spread the adhesive using the manufacturer-recommended method and notched-trowel size. Some adhesives are best spread at an angle to the tile, while others are best spread in overlapping arcs. Be careful not to cover your working lines with adhesive. Keep the appropriate solvent on hand to clean your trowel, and wipe up spills as you work.

Laying the Tile

After spreading the adhesive, press each tile into place with a slight twisting motion to embed it. Do not slide tiles against each other, or you will end up with excess adhesive in the joints. If adhesive does bulk up, clean it out before it hardens. **4–6.**

As you lay the tiles, frequently check their alignment with a level, and make sure you maintain uniform grout spacing. Also check the wall surface with a straightedge periodically to make sure that all the tiles are seated the same way. If you find one that's raised, use more pressure to set it before the adhesive sets up. If you use too much pressure on a tile and embed it below the others, pry it out, butter the back with adhesive, and reset it flush.

When the installation requires a row of cut tiles, do not presume that they will all be the same size. You may have to check each one and adjust its size where the squared-up tile field meets a ceiling that isn't level with the floor or an adjacent wall that isn't plumb with the field.

Finishing

Use a float to spread grout into the joints. Work the float with diagonal sweeps to force the material thoroughly into the seams. **7–8.** Where the tile meets the floor, use a flexible caulk to fill the joint and avoid cracking at this intersection of different materials.

Installing & Finishing Tiles

Tools and Materials   Easy

- Level
- Hammer, nails, and tape
- Notched trowel and adhesive
- Tiles and spacers
- Grout materials

TILE TIP: *To avoid stress cracks, use caulk instead of grout on the floor-level seam.*

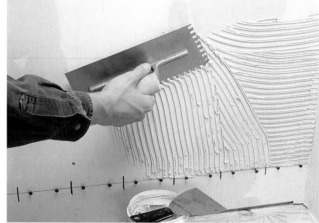

 Prepare to set the field tiles above the nails by spreading adhesive recommended by the tile manufacturer with a notched trowel.

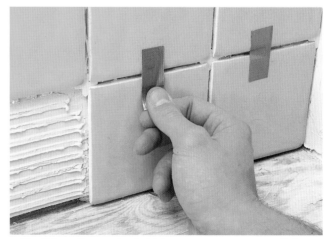

6 *When the main field is secure, you can pull the nails and set the bottom row. Tape prevents sagging so that the floor-level seam won't close up.*

1 Establish a level baseline for the field tiles. Measure up from the floor's high point, allowing for full tiles with grout joints.

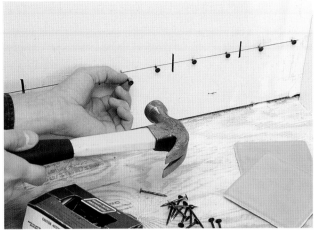

2 One approach is to support the field tiles and prevent sagging with pairs of nails. You install the bottom row after the field tiles have set.

4 Set the field tiles into the adhesive bed with light pressure. Work in a limited area up to a guideline before spreading more adhesive.

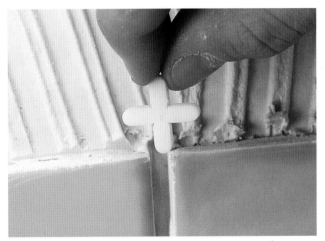

5 Use spacers in grout seams to maintain alignment and to help transfer weight down to the first row, which is supported by the nails.

7 When all the tiles are fixed in place, spread the grout with a float. Use sweeping strokes on diagonals to the tile grid system to fill the seams.

8 Grout leaves a haze even if you finish with a squeegee to remove residue. You need several passes with a clean damp sponge to clear it away.

DESIGN IDEAS: WALLS

Random colors, left, add interest to a tile backsplash.

Stone tiles, below, add an elegant touch to a mudroom wall.

Glass tiles, opposite top left, complement contemporary cabinets.

Mosaic tiles, opposite top right, support a focal-point window.

A step pattern, opposite bottom left, adds drama behind a range.

Border tiles, opposite bottom right, contain a colorful field of tiles.

DESIGN IDEAS: WALLS

Mosaic tiles, left, extend from the wall into the shower.

Metal tiles, above, complement a modern design scheme.

Decorative accents, opposite top left, add sparkle to a subtle design.

Tumbled marble, opposite top right, creates a classical feeling in this bath.

Natural stone, opposite bottom, grounds a room filled with light.

CHAPTER 5

TILING COUNTERTOPS

A ceramic or stone tile counter should outlast hardwood or plastic laminate because it's tougher and won't scorch. Expensive, poured-in-place concrete is probably sturdier than tile, and it's joint-free, too. But it can't offer the variations in color and pattern you get with ceramic or stone tile. Another option is to place ceramic or stone tile insets into another counter material, such as solid surfacing.

To make a durable installation with ceramic tile, you need several layers of material, including a moisture membrane and cement backer board. On many do-it-yourself jobs, trouble stems from leaving them out.

You can adhere tile directly to plywood in dry locations, such as a display counter or tabletop. But for most kitchen and bathroom countertops, you will need either two layers of ¾-inch-thick plywood or a layer of plywood topped with a layer of backer board. The plywood backer-board combination is the preferred method of installation around sinks and drainboards.

Planning the Layout

You can buy tile to meet the needs of a specific counter, or modify a new counter (or a replacement over existing cabinets) to fit your new tile. Modifying the counter is a good approach because it's easy to trim an extra inch or so off a sheet of plywood and backer board. And by deciding on your layout ahead of time, you may be able to create a counter of full tile and edging pieces.

To see how different edging styles will work, the best approach in the confined area of a countertop is to do a dry layout, using spacers to allow for grout seams. Here are some of the design issues to consider.

◆ *Overhangs.* Be sure that the edge treatment provides enough clearance for top drawers in the cabinets and for undercounter appliances. If you run into clearance problems, choose edging tile with a narrow lip.

◆ *Bracing.* Counters with large overhangs, such as serving counters or bars, may require some type of bracing to support the overhang. Even with combined layers of plywood and backer board, you should add braces where needed to make the countertop rigid.

◆ *Sink Installations.* There are several types of sink mounts, including undercounter installation. But the most common type (and the one best suited to do-it-yourself projects) is a self-rimming sink. It has a lip that lies on top of the tile so you don't have to trim tiles against curved metal corners.

◆ *Counter Edging.* There are several ways to trim the counter edge with tile. The most common is to install V-cap matched to the field tiles. It creates a neat border with no grout joint at the outer edge, and covers the backer board and plywood. You also can use bullnose tiles along the edge or even a strip of wood.

◆ *Backsplashes.* Most counter layouts include a backsplash. Take its thickness into account when planning the countertop field: the tiles themselves on drywall, or tiles plus a backer board (and plywood, too, in some cases) in wet areas. You also can use tiles with a cove base to make an easy-cleaning seam.

An island layout blends in with the surroundings when you use the same material on the counter as you do on the floor.

Countertop Construction

Front Edge Options

Wood Trim

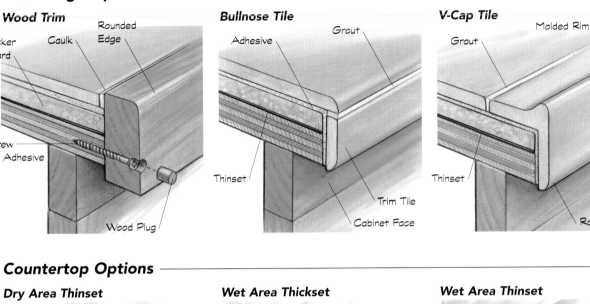

Backer Board
Caulk
Rounded Edge
Screw and Adhesive
Wood Plug

Bullnose Tile

Adhesive
Grout
Thinset
Trim Tile
Cabinet Face

V-Cap Tile

Grout
Molded Rim
Thinset
Rounded Edge

Countertop Options

Dry Area Thinset

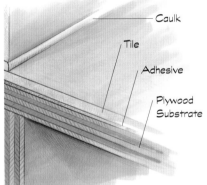

Caulk
Tile
Adhesive
Plywood Substrate

Wet Area Thickset

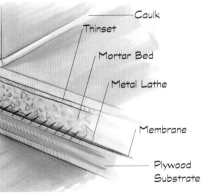

Caulk
Thinset
Mortar Bed
Metal Lathe
Membrane
Plywood Substrate

Wet Area Thinset

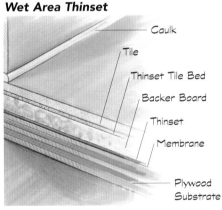

Caulk
Tile
Thinset Tile Bed
Backer Board
Thinset
Membrane
Plywood Substrate

Backsplash Options

Capped Top

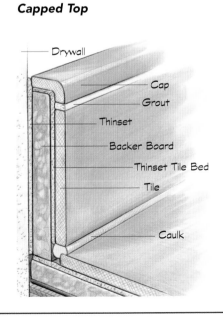

Drywall
Cap
Grout
Thinset
Backer Board
Thinset Tile Bed
Tile
Caulk

Coved Base

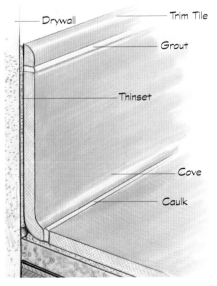

Drywall
Trim Tile
Grout
Thinset
Cove
Caulk

Bullnose Return

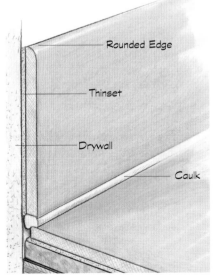

Rounded Edge
Thinset
Drywall
Caulk

Preparing Countertops

Whether you strip the surface material off an old counter or install a new one, the surface has to be level, smooth, and rigid enough to resist movement that could crack grout joints. The best approach is to install a layer of plywood and a layer of cement backer board. The plywood is typically ¾-inch exterior grade with one finished side. The backer board is typically ½ inch thick.

Strengthening Cabinets

Before you install the counter, build in extra strength to resist even slight shifting. On the cabinets, you may need to add shims, construction adhesive, and some screws to make sure that separate components are tied together and locked into the wall studs. On new corner units, such as lazy Susans, you may need to add nailers along the wall. The supporting frame also has to be level.

Strengthening Counters

On a new counter, rip the leftover plywood into long strips about 3 inches wide to reinforce the back of the main panel. **1.** Install the strips with glue and screws along the perimeter, and add cross strips where the counter makes contact with the cabinet partitions. **2.** Construction adhesive at all contact points helps the counter stick to the cabinets. **3.** But you also have to squeeze into the confined spaces and drive screws up through cabinet braces into the bottom of the plywood

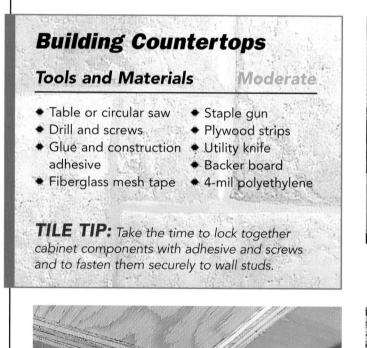

Building Countertops

Tools and Materials   *Moderate*

- Table or circular saw
- Drill and screws
- Glue and construction adhesive
- Fiberglass mesh tape
- Staple gun
- Plywood strips
- Utility knife
- Backer board
- 4-mil polyethylene

TILE TIP: *Take the time to lock together cabinet components with adhesive and screws and to fasten them securely to wall studs.*

1 Rip narrow strips off excess plywood to reinforce the counter. Use a table saw or a circular saw with a straightedge guide.

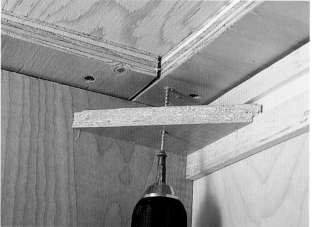

4 Drive holding screws up through corner braces inside the cabinets. Use screws that drive into (but not through) the layers of plywood.

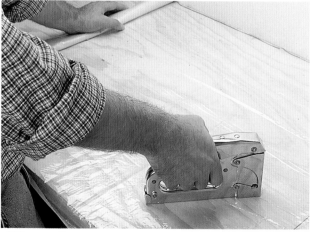

5 Install a moisture-resistant membrane over the plywood counter. You can use 15-lb. felt paper or 4-mil polyethylene sheeting.

counter. **4.** Cabinets generally have either hardware fittings or triangular pieces of wood at the corners.

Counter Options

On counters that won't get wet, you can affix tile directly to the plywood. Use either an epoxy adhesive (generally reserved for installations needing resistance to chemicals and solvents) or the type most homeowners and pros use: organic adhesive, generally called thinset.

But thinset applications that are commonly used on floors and walls are not recommended for kitchen and bathroom counters. Where surfaces get wet, there are two other types of installations. With the old-fashioned approach, generally called thickset, you embed tile in a ¾- to 1-inch-thick bed of metal-reinforced cement mortar leveled over a membrane such as roofing felt. It's a solid system but time-consuming and challenging to float a smooth and level mortar bed.

The more modern wet-area installation starts with a moisture-resistant membrane stapled to the plywood—either 15-pound roofing felt or 4-mil polyethylene, although there are also liquid membranes. **5.** The poly works well because you can drape sheets over the cabinet fronts for protection, and trim the membrane before you tile the counter edge.

Next comes a layer of cement-based backer board set in a bed of thinset combed out in a ribbed pattern with a notched trowel. **6.** You can cut the heavy panels to size with a diamond blade, but it's faster and easier to score and snap them. Use fiberglass mesh tape on the seams. **7.**

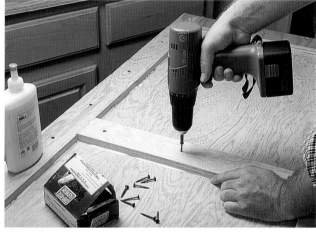

2 Reinforce the plywood counter by attaching the strips along the perimeter with glue and screws. Also install crosspieces over cabinet supports.

3 Use construction adhesive on the cabinet frames to help secure the countertop. Also, cover the partition frames between components.

6 Spread an embedding layer of thinset, and install a layer of cement backer board. Leave about a ⅛-in. gap between the panels.

7 Use fiberglass mesh tape to help bind edge pieces. Also use it on countertop seams, embedded in thinset that fills the gaps between panels.

Making a Sink Cutout

There are several different types of sink installations. You can mount some sinks underneath a counter and trim the edge of the opening with tile. An even more complicated option is to set the sink flush by cutting a rabbet or groove in the surrounding substrate and tiling over the lip of the sink. Both options are quite complicated and are generally taxing for do-it-yourselfers. A better approach is to tile up to the cutout and mount a self-rimming sink on the counter. It has a lip that rests on top of the tile.

In any case, you need to make room for the sink in the plywood and cement backer board. Many sinks come with paper templates. **1–2.** But you can also use the sink itself (turned upside down) to draw the outline. Then measure in from the lip to draw your cut line. If you have problems centering the cutout, measure under the counter to find the center, and drive a nail up through the plywood to mark the spot.

Drill a starter hole for the blade, and cut the plywood with a saber saw. **3–4.** Then lay the membrane, and comb out a bed of thinset with a notched trowel to embed the cement backer board. **5.**

On sink cutouts, it's possible but extremely time-consuming to make a large, carefully shaped hole in backer board to match the plywood cutout below. Instead, run full sheets to the sides of the sink, and fill in front and back with narrow strips of backer board, leaving about a ⅛-inch gap at the seams. **6–7.**

Sink Cutouts

Tools and Materials   *Moderate*

- Measuring tape and framing square
- Drill and ¾" bit
- Saber saw
- Fiberglass mesh tape
- Marker or pencil
- Notched trowel
- Thinset and backer board
- 4-mil polyethylene
- Staple gun

TILE TIP: *Be sure that the cutout location leaves enough room to run supply pipes between the sink and the back of the cabinet.*

1 *Measure carefully to center the cutout. Remember to figure only interior, front-to-back cabinet space where the sink will be housed.*

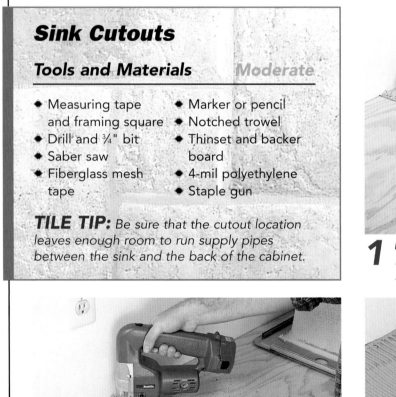

4 *Follow the cut line, working slowly at corners where you rotate the saw. Support the cutout below or install a top cleat as you finish the cut.*

5 *Lay a moisture membrane such as 4-mil polyethylene over the plywood. Then trowel on a bed of thinset adhesive using a notched trowel.*

Tile Tip

Supporting the Cutout

When you cut a sink opening in ¾-inch-thick plywood, the surrounding wood will support the cut for most of the job. But as your saw heads back to the starting point, the cutout section will start to sag. The blade may bind, and the cut piece may tear before you finish the cut.

Solve these problems with a temporary cleat. It should be long enough to cover the cut section plus an inch or so on each side. Two screws will hold the cut section to the cleat, and the ends of the cleat will hold the cutout flush with the counter.

A temporary cleat keeps the sink cutout from falling and causing a ragged break.

2 Use a template with a framing square to position the cutout. If you trace the sink outline, measure in from the lip overhang to mark the actual cut line.

3 Although some saber saws are capable of a plunge cut, it's best to drill a starter hole. Make sure the hole is just inside your cut line.

6 Install sheets of cement backer board up to the edges of the cutout with corrosion-resistant screws. Add narrow strips front and back.

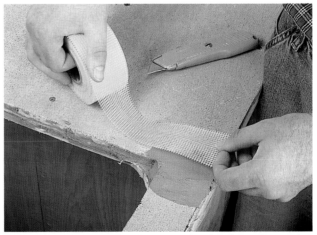

7 Fill the ⅛-in. gaps between backer board panels with thinset, and embed a layer of fiberglass mesh tape over all the panel seams.

Laying the Field Tiles

If you install a new countertop tailored to the size of the field tiles and edging pieces, you should be able to snap guidelines to center up the field and another line to mark your edging tiles. If the counter will include a row of partial tiles, make a dry run with tiles and spacers to determine the best layout.

Try to minimize the number of cuts, but be sure to account for the width of your trim tiles, including all grout joints. If you plan to have a wood edging, butt the whole tiles up to the front edge of the counter surface. Always work from the front of the counter using full edge pieces next to full tiles, and let partial tiles run along the backsplash.

Establishing Working Lines

If you are tiling a rectangular countertop, find and mark the center of the front edge of the countertop. If the counter includes a sink, use it as the center so you will have a symmetrical layout around the rim. If the countertop is open at both ends, adjust the tiles so that cut tiles at each end are equal in width. If the cut tiles are much less than half a tile wide, shift the row of tiles by half a tile width, or adjust the grout joint width.

If the counter is open at only one end, lay out the tiles with full tiles along the open end and cut tiles along the wall at the opposite end. On an island counter, plan the layout with equal border tiles around all the edges.

For an L-shaped countertop, position a tile at the inside corner of the L, and pencil around the edges to mark the starting point. Because this point cannot be adjusted, you may have to cut tiles to fit exposed edges. L-shaped countertops with corner sinks usually involve

odd cuts of tile. In such cases, it is best to start with full tiles at the ends of each leg of the top and work toward the sink opening. With so many options, you can see how important it is to test your plan with a dry run.

Once you have determined the best layout, remove all the dry-laid tiles from the countertop. You can lay field tiles to a line or tack a straight 1×2 guide strip along the front of the countertop. If you are using V-caps or similar trim tiles along exposed edges, mark a line to allow for the width of the trim tiles, and start the field from the line. **1–2.**

Laying the First Course

Apply enough adhesive with a notched trowel to lay several tiles along the front edge. **3.** Lay the key tiles first (center or end tiles, depending on the layout). **4.** Press them gently but firmly in place. Continue filling in tiles on either side of the key tiles, using spacers if necessary, until you cannot fit any more whole tiles. **5.** Check tile alignment frequently with a straightedge or framing square.

Finishing the Field

Spread more adhesive, and continue laying rows of full tiles, working back to the wall as far as you can go without cutting any tiles. You'll find it easiest to stick with full tiles and finish the field before you tackle the partial tiles and the countertop edging.

On large or complex counters where it may take you a while to finish the field, stop periodically to scrape off any adhesive in the cut tile and edging areas. It's more difficult to clear after it sets up, and you need those areas clear and ready for fresh adhesive. Check the field surface with a straightedge to make sure that the tiles are even and level before continuing.

Tile Tip — Scribing to an Uneven Wall

In some locations where you want to install tile, it may not be practical to remodel existing walls and make a corner perfectly square. Wherever surfaces don't meet in a clean, square-edged seam, one option is to scribe the joint.

The idea is to mirror the contour of one surface on another so that the two fit together. To make the contour line, use a compass. Hold the point end against the wall, and draw the tool evenly along so the pencil side of the tool leaves a mark that can guide your saw cut.

Keep the compass points aligned as you mark the contour of the wall onto the plywood.

Installing Field Tiles

Tools and Materials   *Easy*

- Chalk-line box
- Field tile
- Edge tile
- Adhesive
- Notched trowel

TILE TIP: *Remember to allow for a grout seam between the edge tile and the first row of full-size field tiles.*

1 *Use one of the edge tiles to establish a working line for the main field of full tiles. Mark the edge piece at several points along all counter edges.*

2 *Snap chalk guidelines inset from the edges of the counters. Remember to allow for a grout joint between the field tiles and the edge tiles.*

3 *Spread adhesive over the backer board surface using a notched trowel. Start at a point that controls the layout—for example, at an inside corner.*

4 *Embed the first rows of field tiles along your guidelines. Periodically check the alignment of grout seams with a framing square.*

5 *Work your way along the counter to set all the full-size tiles. Check the surface with a straight-edge to be sure the tiles are flat.*

Partial Tile & Edging

If your installation is square, you can make all the partial tiles the same size. But it's wise to check at several points along the field tiles to see whether you need to make slight adjustments. In that case, number the tiles on the back so that you install the unique sizes in the right order. As always, wear goggles or safety glasses when cutting tiles.

Overlap Measurings

There are two easy ways to make overlap measurements. In a straightforward situation where you are using plain tiles in a layout with square boundaries, use one tile. Set it in position and mark the cut line, allowing for grout and caulk seams.**1.** On more complex layouts, set one full tile on top of the adjacent field tile, and another tile on that one, but moved forward to gauge the distance to the wall. (See page 74.) Mark the offset on the tile below, allowing for seams. Then cut and set the tile with the cut edge facing the wall. **2–4.** If the space is narrow, apply adhesive to the back of the tile.

Cutting Around a Sink

Some flush-mounted or inset sinks require curved cuts in all the surrounding tile. Most do-it-yourselfers will find these installations both taxing and very time-consuming. Instead of tiling to the sink, consider the more practical alternative of setting tiles up to the sink cutout and covering the edges with the lip of a self-rimming sink. This way you may be able to make most or all of the trim cuts with a snap cutter, creating a rough outline covered by the sink lip. That's a lot easier than using a nipper to cut row after row of precisely curved tiles.

Installing Edge Tiles

If you used a wood guide to align the field tiles, remove it, and clear any excess adhesive. Fiberglass mesh tape will help adhesive stick to the counter edge, but most people find that it helps to butter the edge tiles before setting them in place. **5–6.**

On L-shaped counters, you normally should begin at the inside corner with a curved piece. Many tile sets are available with molded inside and outside corners. Another option is to cut 45-degree angles on two straight pieces to create miter joints at the corners. **7–8.** Measure these cuts carefully. To maintain grout spacing, you need to align the end of the miter with the corner of the adjacent field tile.

Installing Partial Tiles & Edging

Tools and Materials   *Moderate*

- Full tiles and edging
- Snap cutter
- Notched trowel
- Adhesive
- Fiberglass mesh tape
- Wet saw
- Putty knife

TILE TIP: *If you can't order shaped inside corner pieces, cut mitered sections on a wet saw.*

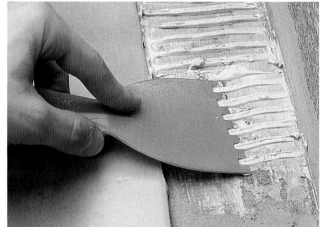

3 *Use a notched trowel to continue the adhesive bed beyond the field tiles. First scrape off any dry adhesive spread when you set the field.*

6 *Set the edge tiles to align with the grout joints of the field tiles. Work the edging pieces slightly side to side to embed them firmly.*

1 To mark a partial tile, set a full tile so that it overlaps one of the field tiles and butts against the wall or backsplash. Mark where the two tiles meet.

2 Use a snap cutter to score the tile surface, and snap it on your mark. Remember to allow space for grout joints between tiles.

4 Embed partial tiles in the adhesive with firm pressure. You may want to use a straightedge to be sure the cut tiles are flush with the field.

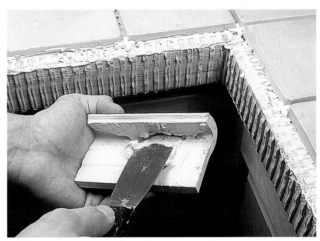

5 Butter the backs of V-cap or other edge pieces with adhesive. Fiberglass mesh tape on the counter edges will improve the bond.

7 To make an inside corner out of straight edging tiles, cut them at a 45 deg. angle to make a miter joint, allowing for a grout seam.

8 Set the second mitered corner piece firmly in place. If adhesive bulges out and fills the seam, clear the excess to make room for grout.

Installing a Backsplash

There are several ways to build a backsplash. In a dry area, you can simply adhere the tiles to the wall. In wet areas, it's wiser to provide the same kind of protection you give the countertop by installing backer board. Depending on the size of the tile, you may want to install backer board only, to leave a narrow top edge. You can build a thicker backsplash with plywood and backer board (like most counters), and install a larger cap piece.

Installing Backer Board

On installations with just backer board, start by scoring and snapping a sheet to a height that will work with full tile and a top row of cap tiles. In almost all cases (unless there is a window or cabinet in the way), you should not have to use partial tiles on a backsplash. You can spread thinset on the wall, but it's easier to apply an even coat on the back of the backer board. After you set the panel firmly in place, secure it with corrosion-resistant screws driven into the studs. If the wall isn't flat, driving screws could deform the backer board. You can build a more stable surface by installing plywood and backer board.

Installing Plywood

If you're installing a new plywood counter, it's easy to join it to a solid plywood backsplash and set both pieces in place at the same time. **1–7.** This approach provides a very solid connection along the key seam where the counter joins the wall. You can join the backsplash to

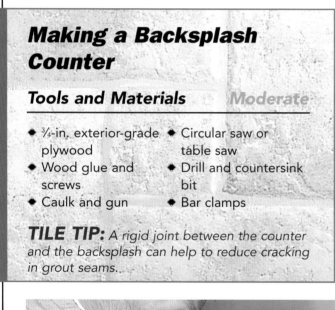

Making a Backsplash Counter

Tools and Materials   Moderate

- ¾-in. exterior-grade plywood
- Wood glue and screws
- Caulk and gun
- Circular saw or table saw
- Drill and countersink bit
- Bar clamps

TILE TIP: A rigid joint between the counter and the backsplash can help to reduce cracking in grout seams.

1 Rip strips of plywood about 3 in. wide to reinforce the edges of the counter. If you don't have a table saw, use a circular saw with a guide.

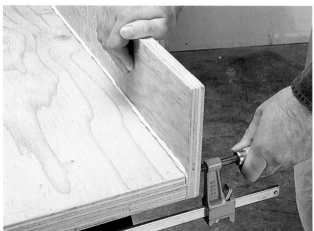

4 Hold the backsplash panel to the counter with clamps. You can use a square to align the pieces before fully tightening the clamps.

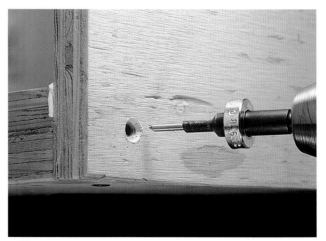

5 Predrill through the backsplash panel into the reinforced plywood counter. Use a combination bit to make a countersink at the same time.

the counter with glue and screws and take the extra step of sealing the seam with a liberal bead of silicone. If any moisture gets through the tile, this waterproof seam can prevent the backsplash from separating.

Installing Plywood & Backer Board

This is the system used for maximum durability on wet-area counters. It also provides a solid and water-resistant base for a backsplash. If you install the counter and back-splash as a connected unit, you can coat the back of the backer board or the face of the plywood before screwing the layer of backer board in place. The double layer back-splash will be very rigid.

Treat the exposed edges of plywood and backer board on the backsplash the way you treat them on the edge of the counter. Wrap them in fiberglass mesh tape before installing the cap trim.

Planning Backsplash Tile

You can use tile with a cove base on the first course of backsplash tile if you have allowed room for the curved base with the counter tiles. If tiles in the last row on the counter are cut, the joint will look better if you cover the cut edges with full tiles on the backsplash. But be sure to leave a full-size seam.

You can finish the top course of a backsplash with bullnose tiles or V-cap-style trim tiles that wrap over the top edge. Another option is to extend the backsplash up the wall to the bottom edge of a cabinet. You can trim an extended backsplash with tile or wood trim.

2 Cut the strips to fit along the counter edges and where the counter crosses cabinet framing. Secure the strips with glue and screws.

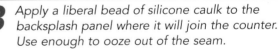

3 Apply a liberal bead of silicone caulk to the backsplash panel where it will join the counter. Use enough to ooze out of the seam.

6 Drive screws about every 6 in. to secure the back-splash. The pressure should squeeze the caulk into a gasket that waterproofs the seam.

7 Once the caulk sets up, peel away the excess, trimming where necessary. Then you can install the counter with the backsplash attached.

Backsplash Design Options

One Tile & Cap

The easiest and quickest installation uses the same basic grid as the countertop tiles, and simply extends the grid one course onto the wall. Remember to leave a standard-width seam between the backsplash and the counter. Where you may get some movement between the two components, use caulk in this joint instead of grout.

Dry-Area Prep Work. In dry areas you can apply tile adhesive directly to the drywall and set the tile in place.

Wet-Area Prep Work. In wet areas, cut backer board to fit the tile and cap, comb the back of the panel with thinset, and screw with corrosion-resistant fasteners to the wall studs.

1 Use a notched trowel to spread adhesive from the counter to a top guideline on the wall. You can add tape to keep a clean line.

Multiple Rows & Cap

Use multiple rows of tile or combinations of sizes and shapes that create a decorative accent for the countertop. Some tiles are sold in decorative sets, such as a group of four pretrimmed tiles designed to fit around a center medallion. Square-edged tiles in sets need a cap tile on the top row.

Color Contrast. If you change color between the countertop and the backsplash, maintain the same grout spacing to tie the areas together. Create a more decorative look by using contrasting colors within the backsplash grid—for example, by matching the counter color with the medallion tile.

Spacing. If tiles tend to sag on the adhesive, use temporary spacers to maintain spacing.

1 Install pattern sets, pretrimmed for insert tiles, to create a more decorative backsplash. Inserts have to be centered to maintain grout spacing.

Multiple Trim Strips

When you begin to combine basic elements, such as single rows and tile sets with accents, you can create many variations. You can add contrasting colors to the mix, and decorative tiles with an embossed pattern or picture. More complex layouts call for careful planning. Larger backsplash installations can also support intermediate trim strips.

Dry Layout. Test your design with a dry layout. You can temporarily tape sample pieces to a board so that you can see how the design looks on the wall.

Staggering Joints. Lining up vertical grout seams on a large backsplash emphasizes height. Offsetting intermediate trim strips so they bridge the seams between full tiles emphasizes width.

1 Intermediate trim strips separate different design elements on a backsplash wall. They also tie together different colors and shapes.

2 Set the row of backsplash tiles into the adhesive, but leave a standard seam along the bottom. You may need spacers to keep the tiles from sagging.

3 Cover the top edges of full backsplash tiles with a cap tile. Another option is to use tile with a finished, bullnose edge on top.

2 Press pattern insets into place by hand. You may want to use a straightedge to make sure they are flush with the surrounding tiles.

3 A larger backsplash with a more complex pattern can support a larger, S-shaped cap. You also can make caps from cut sections of bullnose tiles.

2 Horizontal trim strips provide a secondary baseline to support a row of decorative tiles with different colors and patterns.

3 When you combine different design elements, it generally looks best to use narrow trim strips in the pattern and wide trim on the cap.

Finishing a Backsplash

In most cases, you should allow the tile adhesive to set for an hour or two. (Check the manufacturer's recommendations.) If you grout too soon, some of the tiles could shift. Remove tile spacers, and use a damp cloth to clean any adhesive off the tile surface. Also, check for adhesive buildup in the joints that could get in the way of grout, and use a screwdriver or narrow chisel to scrape it away. **1.**

Generally, you need to allow the adhesive to cure for at least 24 hours before grouting. If you have used unglazed tiles, coat them before grouting with a sealant recommended by the tile manufacturer. Be sure that the sealer has cured fully before applying the grout.

Applying the Grout

Mix the grout according to the manufacturer's instructions, and apply it with a rubber float or squeegee, working diagonally across the joints. **2–3.** You'll need to make several passes to pack the grout firmly into every joint and eliminate air bubbles.

When the grout becomes firm, use a damp sponge or a squeegee to remove excess from the tile surface. Then shape the grout joints using a striking tool. **4–5.** (A toothbrush handle, spoon, or something similar will work.) Clean off the tiles again with a damp sponge. **6.** Then wipe away the final haze with a clean, damp cloth. In most cases, the grout will take several days to harden completely. Then you may want to protect the seams by applying a grout sealer. **7.**

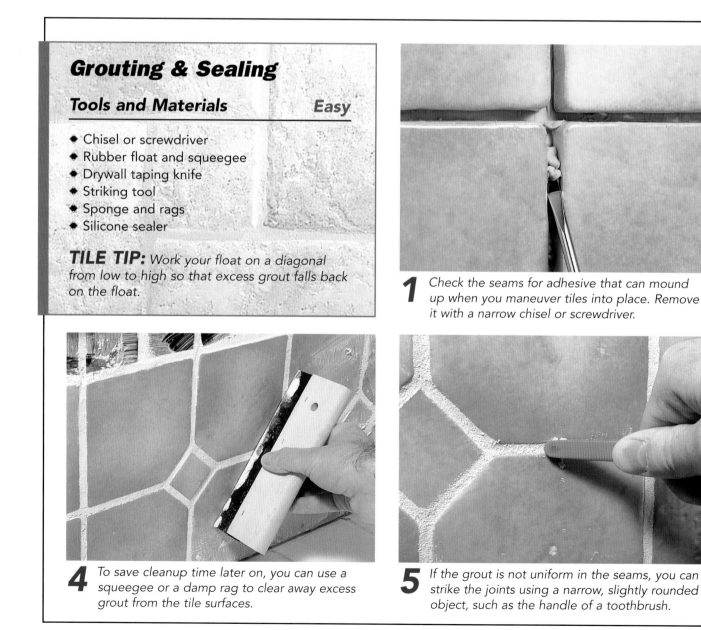

Grouting & Sealing

Tools and Materials   Easy

- Chisel or screwdriver
- Rubber float and squeegee
- Drywall taping knife
- Striking tool
- Sponge and rags
- Silicone sealer

TILE TIP: Work your float on a diagonal from low to high so that excess grout falls back on the float.

1 Check the seams for adhesive that can mound up when you maneuver tiles into place. Remove it with a narrow chisel or screwdriver.

4 To save cleanup time later on, you can use a squeegee or a damp rag to clear away excess grout from the tile surfaces.

5 If the grout is not uniform in the seams, you can strike the joints using a narrow, slightly rounded object, such as the handle of a toothbrush.

A collection of different tiles with related colors and patterns is tied together with a strip of trim tiles. This kind of random installation, which might be overwhelming on a countertop, works quite well on a backsplash.

2 Mix the grout to a mudlike consistency (according to manufacturer's recommendations), and load it onto a rubber float.

3 Work the float on a diagonal to the tile joints to fill the seams. If you sweep the float upward, excess grout will fall back on the float.

6 Wipe down the wall with a clean, damp sponge, rinsing regularly. After each cleaning (you'll need more than one) there will be less of a surface haze.

7 After polishing the wall with a soft cloth to remove the final haze, you can protect grout in wet areas by applying a liquid silicone sealer.

Installing a Mosaic Tile Vanity Top

Most common mosaic tiles come in sheets, often 12 inches square, with the individual tiles glued to a mesh backer. This makes installing these small tiles much easier. The job goes quicker because of the size of the sheets, and it looks better because the grout joints are so consistent. Except for this mesh backer, mosaics are generally installed the same way as other ceramic tiles. You begin with a cement backer-board base, followed by a coat of thinset mortar. The tiles are then laid in the mortar, and when the mortar is dry, the gaps between the tiles are filled with grout.

Mosaic Tile Layout

Layout is just as important for mosaics as it is for other types of tile. In some situations, such as the vanity top we show here, layout can be very easy. Because this free-standing vanity had plenty of room around it, we laid out our counter to fit the tile instead of the other way around. By just adding ½ inch to the width and depth of the top, we were able to use standard edge trim pieces and full tiles across the entire top. This saved a lot of cutting and made for a much better-looking job.

Once your tile installation is complete, reinstall the vanity sink. Before dropping it in place, run a thick bead of clear silicone caulk around the perimeter of the sink cutout. Drop the sink in place. Let the caulk dry; then trim excess caulk flush to the sink using a utility knife.

Mosaic Tile Vanity Top

Tools and Materials

- Power drill, screws
- Screwdriver
- Rubber-faced trowel
- Tile nippers
- Mosaic tile sheets
- Hammer, rubber mallet
- Circular saw, saber saw
- Notched trowel
- Thinset mortar
- Edge trim tiles

TILE TIP: Tile vanity tops sometimes omit a tiled backsplash. A good replacement is a straight piece of knot-free pine. Chamfer the top and side edges, prime, and paint with a high-gloss latex paint.

1 Remove the existing sink, and cover the vanity top with a piece of cement backer board. Mark and cut out the sink opening using a jigsaw.

4 Carefully install the edge tiles first, starting at the corners. The grout lines on the edge tiles should match those of the mosaic sheets.

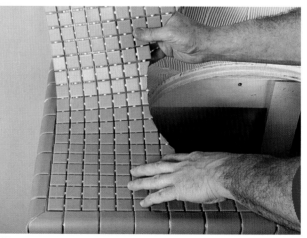

5 Start installing the mosaic sheets at the perimeter, and work toward the sink hole. Carefully lower the sheet into the mortar.

Installing Broken Mosaic Tiles

To create your own distinctive mosaic tiles, just put a variety of different colored tile into a plastic storage bag, and break them with a hammer. Try for pieces that are about 1 in. wide.

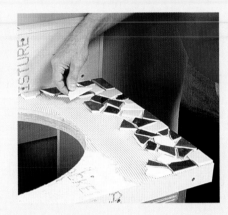

Spread some thinset mortar on your vanity top, and push the broken tile into the mortar in a random pattern. Keep the top as flat as possible to make grouting easier later.

2 Temporarily tape a few trim pieces in place; then determine the most attractive layout for the mosaic tile.

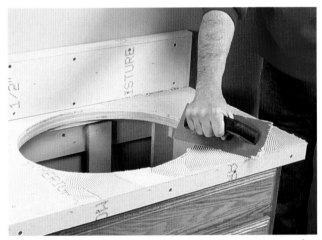

3 Spread thinset mortar on the edges and top of the backer board. Apply the mortar uniformly, following the manufacturer's directions.

6 Once all the sheets are installed, carefully tap the sheets into the mortar using a scrap wood block and a rubber mallet or hammer.

7 Once the mortar has cured, mix up some tile grout according to the manufacturer's directions. Spread it over the tiles using a rubber trowel.

DESIGN IDEAS: COUNTERTOPS

Colorful tiles, *opposite, used on a counter and backsplash.*

Tile landing spot, *above, inset next to a range.*

Elegant tile design, *right, complements a distinctive faucet.*

Distinctive trim tiles, *below, enhance a vanity top.*

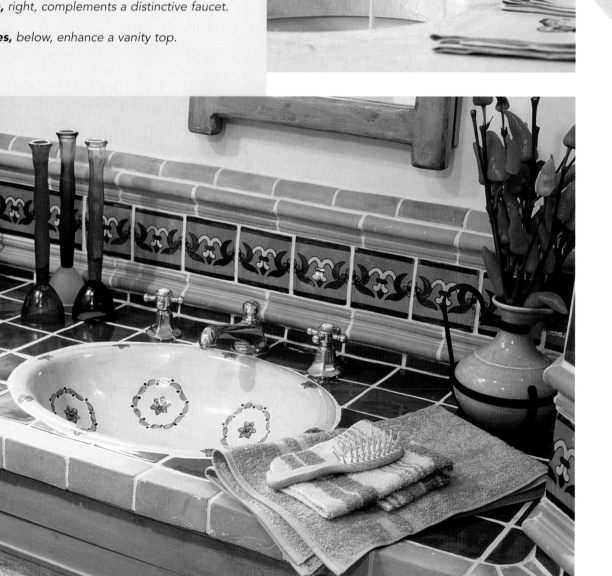

DESIGN IDEAS: COUNTERTOPS

A distinctive vanity top, above left, helps set the mood in this powder room.

Mosaic tiles, left, add a rich appealing touch to a makeup vanity. Note the curved edge to the left of the photo.

Green and white tiles, above, combine to set the tone for this retro bathroom.

Distinctive stone tiles, opposite, are used to create an unusual vanity area.

CHAPTER 6

■■■

TILING TUBS & SHOWERS

Few materials are as suitable for showers and tub surrounds as tile. Smooth, highly glazed tiles are easy to clean, and the glaze can stand up to abrasive and chemical cleaners. If you are tiling a shower floor, select a vitreous or impervious glazed tile with a slip-resistant surface.

Because a tub surround or shower enclosure is subjected to water and steam, both the tile and backing must be watertight. For maximum protection against seepage, you need a water-resistant adhesive such as latex thinset. Some grouts contain additives that help prevent the growth of mildew, which can be a chronic problem in poorly ventilated bathrooms.

Where tile joins a tub, you need the stability and water resistance of cement-based backer board on the surrounding walls. You also need to make a solid tub installation. If you use a fiberglass or acrylic unit, reduce flexing (which can open tile seams) by packing the base in a supporting material of quick-drying plaster. With tubs or spas that rest on tiled platforms, it's important to build a substantial supporting floor for the unit.

Preparing the Site

In a new house or addition, you can prepare tub and shower enclosures that are square and level, and build in modern, watertight substrates. In an existing house, the first step often is to remove old tile and the thick bed of mortar beneath it. This is always messy and sometimes potentially dangerous, so you should wear safety goggles, a dust mask, work gloves, and a heavy long-sleeved shirt as you demolish old wall surfaces.

Removing Old Tile

To start, protect the work area with sheets of plywood and a tarp or drop cloth. Use a sledgehammer and cold chisel to remove the tiles, starting from the top course and working downward toward the tub or shower pan. **1–3.** You may want to place a large bucket directly beneath the tiles to catch them. If the tiles are set in mortar, you also may need to snip through reinforcing mesh to release chunks from the wall. If you plan to reuse the tub, install extra protection, including some kind of padding such as folded-over blankets under the tarp.

When you remove tiles from drywall, some of the paper facing usually tears off, exposing the gypsum core. Once this happens, either remove the panel or install another layer of backing material over it. **4–5.** If you find plaster or conventional drywall around a tub or shower, cover it or replace it with backer board.

Fixtures

In most cases, you need the rough plumbing in place before you start a tile installation. If you're installing a prefabricated shower pan that comes with a drain hole, you may want to set it in place and mark the subfloor first. That way you can adjust the plumbing connections a bit to get a perfect fit. More often, walls have short pipe stems protruding. You can tile close to them without making exact cuts because the pipes are covered by escutcheon plates. If you're re-tiling an area, remove handles and trim pieces, and protect threaded ends during the work.

Tile Tip   Investigating Water Damage

Cracked grout, extensive mold stains, loose tiles, and a surface that flexes when you push on it are all likely indicators of water damage in the supporting wall. Sometimes you can pop off loose tiles, let the surface dry, and re-tile the area. But when damage is more than skin deep and the wall seems weak, you need to investigate further.

Often you don't see dampness on the wall surface; just the results of swelling and shifting that may be caused by a leak. You may need to remove a few loose tiles to see whether the trouble is due to pipe problems or condensation. If drywall under the tile is spongy and flaky, you should strip it from the studs. The idea is to keep digging until you reach the limit of the damage. If the wood framing is rotten, it needs to go as well. Otherwise, it's only a question of time before the shifting or swelling disrupts your new tile.

Scrape a sharp knife across a damp and discolored stud. If the wood surface is sound underneath, dry out the stud and leave it in place.

Dig in the point of a knife to see whether the wood is rotten. If you can dig out crumbling wood, the best course of action is to replace the stud.

Removing Old Tile

Tools and Materials   Easy

- Power drill and masonry bit
- Sledge hammer
- Cold chisel
- Pry bar
- Large bucket and padding (optional)

TILE TIP: *If you find standard drywall behind old tile around a tub or shower, the best plan is to remove it and install cement-based backer board in its place.*

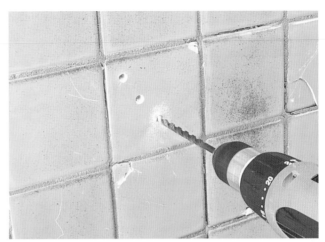

1 *If you have trouble getting started, drill a few holes in a tile with a masonry bit. The holes create a fault line that makes the tile easy to break.*

2 *Use a cold chisel to split off sections of tile and to chop out grout. Remember to wear safety glasses to guard against flying chips of tile.*

3 *Once you have an exposed edge of tile and adhesive (or mortar) to work on, use the flat end of a pry bar to pop tiles off the wall.*

4 *Pull the nails in damaged drywall so that you can release the sheets from the studs. It pays to replace drywall with cement-based backer board.*

5 *Old drywall often breaks, leaving pieces stuck to the studs with nails. You need to remove any nail shanks that could crack the backer board.*

Planning the Job

If you are building a shower stall or bathtub enclosure from scratch, the easiest approach is to install a prefabricated unit. With showers, you can use a pan (usually made of fiberglass) that has a hole for the drain connections and short walls with flanges. Set the pan into your enclosure, and install backer board on the walls that rest on top of the flanges. With tubs, follow the same basic procedure. You may need to pack a bedding material (usually a fast-setting, lightweight plaster) around the tub base to stabilize the unit and prevent flexing.

Tiling a Shower Pan

If you want to tile a shower floor as well as the walls, you can buy a pre-tiled pan, or build your own base with a mortar bed that slopes to a central drain. For backup protection, mortar installations are troweled over a waterproof membrane. You can install a mortar bed over an exterior grade plywood subfloor, or use concrete over an existing slab. For a do-it-yourselfer with limited experience, it's wise to have an experienced contractor install the pan. Then you can complete the enclosure on your own.

Closing Off the Shower

You can try to keep water in a shower enclosure simply by hanging a curtain across the opening. But most showers look better and leak less with a fitted glass door. This approach does make tiling more complicated.

Generally you need to build stub walls on either side of the opening and a curb along the front edge. Stub walls are framed in before the tile and backing are installed. They make a neat opening but create more tiled corners and edges than a basic tiled box closed off with a curtain.

Although some shower doors can be adjusted slightly for width, you need to plan a door opening very carefully. The framing has to leave room for a layer of backer board and tile. Also in the stub framing include a curb that rises higher than the pan itself. The overall height of the opening normally isn't crucial because you don't need to close in the top of the door. But try to plan the curb height to minimize the number of cuts and partial tiles.

If you decide not to use stub walls, the front edge of the fiberglass pan serves as a threshold to contain water. In every case, it's wise to set blocks of framing and backer board in place and try a test layout.

Enclosure Construction

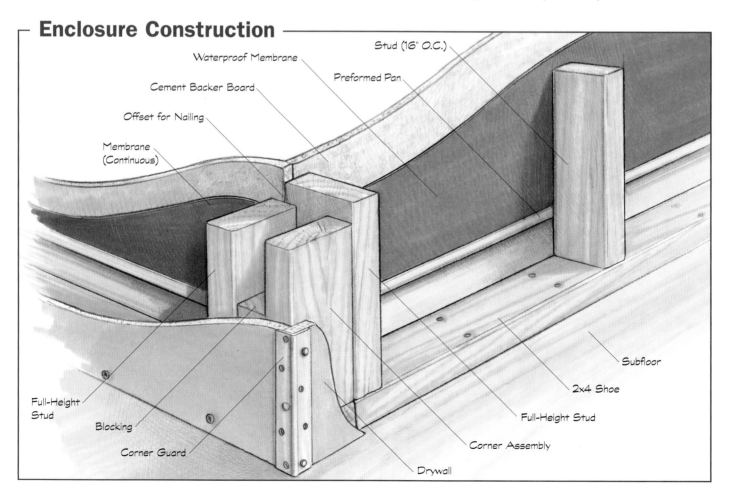

Stud (16" O.C.)

Waterproof Membrane

Cement Backer Board

Preformed Pan

Offset for Nailing

Membrane (Continuous)

Full-Height Stud

Blocking

Corner Guard

Drywall

Corner Assembly

Full-Height Stud

2x4 Shoe

Subfloor

Designing the Enclosure

In conventional tub and shower surrounds, the tile usually extends from the top edges of the tub or shower pan to 6 or 8 inches above the shower head. Of course, you can tile all the way to the ceiling, too. Around tubs without shower heads, you can install a tiled backsplash extending a foot or two above the tub.

In situations where the walls extend beyond the sides of the tub and you do not want to tile the entire wall, you'll need to edge the installation with bullnose tile. This is a good spot to add an extra strip of trim tiles. For example, you might add several rows of full tiles extending up from the edge of the tub, and top them with narrow trim strips in a contrasting color before adding another row of full tiles and bullnose trim.

Instead of aligning the outermost row with the edge of the tub, it often looks neater to extend the backsplash along the wall by a tile or two, and run those columns down to floor level.

You can also tile the ceiling above a tub or shower enclosure, but the job is very difficult for beginners. You need to use a fast-setting adhesive as well as a plywood form supported by long wooden props to keep the tiles in place until the adhesive sets up.

On small-scale sheet tile you can remove a few units and substitute a contrasting color to create a pattern.

Enclosure Floor Membranes

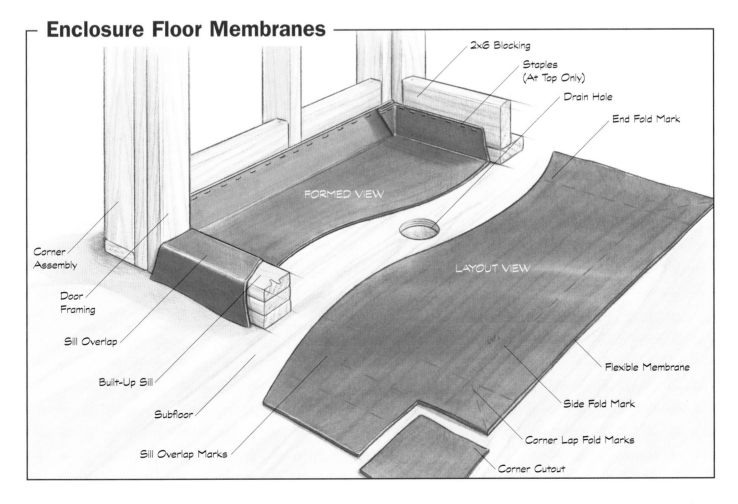

- 2x6 Blocking
- Staples (At Top Only)
- Drain Hole
- End Fold Mark
- FORMED VIEW
- LAYOUT VIEW
- Corner Assembly
- Door Framing
- Sill Overlap
- Built-Up Sill
- Subfloor
- Sill Overlap Marks
- Flexible Membrane
- Side Fold Mark
- Corner Lap Fold Marks
- Corner Cutout

Installing Prefab Pans

If you use a prefabricated shower pan, tiling a shower enclosure becomes a doable do-it-yourself project. You don't have to float a mortar bed on the floor that slopes down to a drain. You can tile the flat wall surfaces down to the pan without having to deal with cove tiles at the base and aligning wall joints with floor joints.

You do need to build the enclosure to suit the size of the pan. **1.** To make your planning and layout more accurate, you may want to buy the pan before framing. That way you can be sure that the unit will fit. Also, prefabricated pans generally come with a drain hole already drilled. You could do all the rough plumbing ahead of time, and hope that you have the drain at dead center of the enclosure. But it's safer to set the pan in place after the framing is done, and mark the drain location on the subfloor through the hole in the pan. **2–4.**

Even when you use a prefabricated pan, there are many elements to coordinate. If only one measurement is off the intended layout, such as an off-center drain line, you might have to adjust the framing and move the pan, which could throw off your tile layout on the enclosure walls. If you're considering a custom enclosure with a floated floor, remember that it will be even more complex and require more thorough planning.

Framing Support

You can use standard framing lumber and techniques to build a tub or shower enclosure. The basic frame consists

Setting a Shower Pan

Tools and Materials   Easy

- Shower pan
- Hammer and nails
- Measuring tape and spirit level
- Drill, screwdriver bit, and screws
- Framing square
- 2×6s for blocking
- Saber saw
- Rubber mallet and pencil
- Backer board, thinset, and fiberglass tape

TILE TIP: *Some pans have narrow ledges for thin surround panels. For tile and backer board, you need a pan with a deep ledge.*

1 Check the enclosure to be sure the framing is square. Add extra studs if necessary to provide adequate nailing surfaces in the corners.

4 Set the pan in place, align the drain holes, and check for level. You need a level pan and square walls to avoid an irregular tile layout.

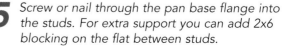

5 Screw or nail through the pan base flange into the studs. For extra support you can add 2×6 blocking on the flat between studs.

of a 2×4 laid flat on the floor, studs 16 inches on center, and double 2×4s across the top of the wall. Select the straightest and driest studs possible to build your walls. Wet lumber can twist enough to disrupt tile joints even when the frame is covered with cement-based backer board. **5–7.**

It's important to provide adequate nailing surfaces for the backer board, so don't scrimp on lumber at the corners. If you use ½-inch backer board, remember that the thickness of the piece on one side of the corner will reduce the available nailing surface on the other.

When the pan is in place and the drain flange is attached, conduct a water test. Plug the drain and flood the pan with water to be sure that the drain seal is working. Protect the pan and drain when you tile the walls.

You can create a custom built-in look by carrying tile details on bath walls into the shower enclosure.

2 On new construction, you can mark the drain hole and run plumbing to suit. Over existing drains you must adjust the enclosure to center the pan.

3 After removing the pan, drill a starting hole, and cut through the subfloor using a saber saw or reciprocating saw to get access to the drainpipe.

6 With the pan in position over the drainpipe, follow manufacturer's recommendations for installing the drain gasket.

7 Apply cement-based backer board to the studs with corrosion-resistant screws or nails. Seal and tape the seams before adding adhesive and tiling.

Installing a Mortar-Bed Floor

This is one of the most difficult types of tile installations, and it's often best left to the pros. Although parts of the job are common to all tile work, a few areas are unfamiliar to do-it-yourselfers.

Framing Details

There are three keys to this part of the project. First, install blocking between the surrounding joists to provide continuous support for the base. Make the blocking several inches higher than the mortar bed so that you can run the membrane up the wall and under the bottom edge of the backer board.

Second, install a wood curb made of three 2×4s to form the front of the shower base. You can also form the curb space and pour in reinforced mortar as an extension of the floor. But this approach is more difficult, and you have no way to make the slight adjustments needed to keep the tile layout symmetrical.

Third, add extra framing to make the floor absolutely rigid. It pays to double up joists under a shower (and even more so under a tub) and to use ¾-inch exterior-grade plywood for the underlayment.

Flexible Membranes

You can make a waterproof pan out of lead, copper, and other materials. But the most modern and practical material is a heavy, flexible membrane made of chlorinated polyethylene (CPE) or polyvinyl chloride (PVC). It is flexible enough to fold snugly into corners. Many suppliers also provide shaped patches to provide extra waterproofing at complex joints. Before tiling, seal the drain and fill the pan with water for 24 hours to test for leaks.

Drain Fixtures

Standard fixture drains have a single collar on the surface (usually set in silicone sealant) that threads onto the rough plumbing to finish and seal the drain area. Drains in tiled showers are different. A typical unit has three separate parts. The lower flange connects to the drainpipe and includes bolt holes for the upper flange. Typically, the top of the lower flange rests flush with the subfloor. You cut the flexible membrane to allow drainage, and clamp down its edges in sealant beds by bolting on the upper flange. This part has a stem that rises to the level of your mortar and weep holes to drain any moisture in the mortar bed. It is topped by a finished chrome screen.

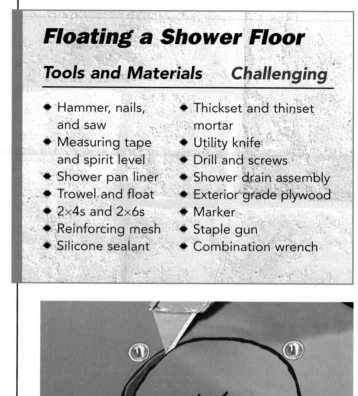

Floating a Shower Floor

Tools and Materials **Challenging**

- Hammer, nails, and saw
- Measuring tape and spirit level
- Shower pan liner
- Trowel and float
- 2×4s and 2×6s
- Reinforcing mesh
- Silicone sealant
- Thickset and thinset mortar
- Utility knife
- Drill and screws
- Shower drain assembly
- Exterior grade plywood
- Marker
- Staple gun
- Combination wrench

3 Cut the membrane with a utility knife to install the drain. Most drains have two parts that you bolt together to sandwich the membrane.

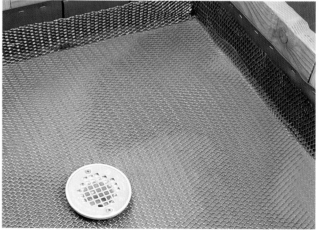

6 Embed galvanized reinforcing mesh in the mortar, and bend up an inch or so on the walls. The metal adds strength to the masonry base.

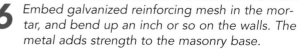

1 Build a curb across the front of the enclosure, and add blocking on the flat between the studs. Add another layer of underlayment over the subfloor.

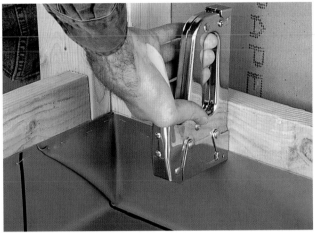

2 Carefully measure and rough-trim the shower pan liner. Fold over extra material at the corners and secure only the top edge all around with staples.

4 Attach the upper drain assembly to the lower assembly with bolts. Sandwich the membrane between the assemblies in sealant beds.

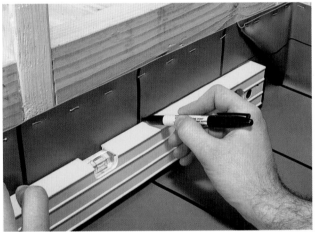

5 Strike lines on the wall to create a slope to the drain of about ¼ in. per foot. Apply about half the final thickness of mortar, establishing the slope.

7 Apply the rest of the mortar, mixed to the consistency of wet sand. Use a trowel to smooth out corners and a large float to smooth the slopes.

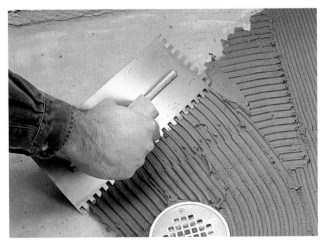
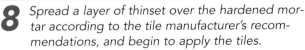

8 Spread a layer of thinset over the hardened mortar according to the tile manufacturer's recommendations, and begin to apply the tiles.

Setting Tub & Shower Tile

Basic installation is the same on shower walls as it is on other walls. Because of the wet conditions, however, there is a difference in the use of substrates.

Greenboard & Backer Board

On dry-area walls, you can tile directly over standard wallboard. In showers, you need cement-based backer board or specially treated, water-resistant drywall, generally called greenboard.

Backer board is the best choice because it will not deteriorate when wet, while greenboard eventually may soften and give way. But you should check local building codes for details. Many now require a waterproof membrane between the studs and backing material.

Working Lines

Establish your vertical and horizontal working lines on the back wall because it is the most visible. Then project the horizontal lines to the adjoining walls, and center vertical working lines on each wall to be tiled. Ideally, you want a course of full tiles around the shower pan, leaving a gap for mildew-resistant silicone, acrylic, or latex tub-and-tile caulk to allow for expansion and contraction. Because you will be working in a small area, tile the back wall first. Then fill in the sidewalls, stub walls, and threshold. This way you're not likely to disturb tiles that have already been set.

The Main Vertical Line. Center the vertical working line on the back wall. **1–2.** Then establish the vertical lines on the side walls. The installation will look best if the cut tiles on the inside corners of the end walls are equal in width to those on the back wall. If you are tiling a shower enclosure with stub walls, plan on cutting tiles to fit around the threshold to maintain continuous grout lines. If possible, adjust the layout lines to avoid extremely narrow-cut tiles around the opening.

The Main Horizontal Line. If the tub or shower pan is level to within ⅛ inch, locate the horizontal working line by leveling from the high point of the rim. Measure up the wall the width of one whole tile plus enough room for a grout joint on top and a caulk joint next to the pan. **3–5.** A slight variation in the gap between the rim and first course of tiles will not be noticeable after it is caulked.

Where wall tiles *meet a tub, shower pan, or even a window frame, seal the seam with caulk instead of grout.*

Installing the Tile

Tools and Materials   Moderate

- Measuring tape and chalk-line box
- Spirit level and pencil
- Battens and screws
- Power drill and screwdriver bit
- Thinset adhesive and notched trowel
- Rubber grout float, spacers, and masking tape

TILE TIP: Try to plan the layout so that shower doors will mount over full tiles.

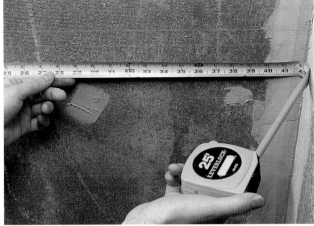

1 Measure the back wall of the enclosure to find the center. Be sure to do a test layout to see how partial tiles will fall in the corners.

2 Use a chalk-line box to snap the main vertical working line on the back of the enclosure. That wall is important because it is the most visible.

3 Check with a level to find the high point, and then measure up one full tile plus a grout joint at the top and bottom of the tile.

4 Make level marks, and snap the horizontal working line around the enclosure. If the base isn't exactly level, the discrepancy will be in the grout joint.

5 To support the field tiles and prevent sagging, you can install a temporary plywood batten with screws driven into the enclosure studs.

Continued on page 144

Continued from page 143

6 Use a notched trowel to spread adhesive up to the lines. For the best bond, spread adhesive with the flat edge first.

7 Rake back across the adhesive with the notched edge of the trowel. The adhesive should have a recommended notch size.

8 Set full tiles along the horizontal working line, using spacers to maintain even grout seams. You can complete full rows or work a pyramid shape.

9 Set a full tile on the last tile in the main field to mark the corner pieces, allowing for a grout seam in the corner. Trim them using a snap cutter.

10 Rake out adhesive for the bottom row, and set the tiles. Use temporary spacers or tape to keep the tiles centered.

11 When the adhesive sets up (usually overnight), you can use a rubber float to spread grout into the seams.

Applying Adhesive

Apply adhesive on the surface using the straight side of your trowel to spread the mix and the notched side to comb it out into even ribs. **6–7.**

To keep the job moving smoothly, complete one full wall before starting on the next. If you apply adhesive to more than one wall before setting the tiles, the adhesive may start to set up or skin over. To see how much working time you have, check the adhesive label. If you are covering a small area of the wall, it is often possible to cover the entire surface with adhesive and lay the tiles before the adhesive sets up or loses its tack. On larger surfaces, fill in small sections at a time.

Installing Tile Supports

Standard working procedure is to install the second course first and the first course last. This allows you to work to a dead level line even if the shower pan lip is slightly out of level. Later on you can go back to the first course and set the tiles with a grout space above and a caulk space below.

To keep the field of tiles from sagging as you work, you may want to install a batten (a straight-edged strip of plywood as in Step **5** or a 1×2) or a row of nails along the level working line. Once the field tiles are set, remove the batten and set the first course of tiles. **8–10.**

Before you start setting tiles, it pays to double-check the space below the working line. Remember that you need to allow for a grout line between the first and second course and at least ⅛ in. for a caulked seam along the shower pan.

Tiling Sequence

Start by laying the first tiles against the vertical layout line, and work the field out to each corner. As always, it's wise to make periodic checks with a straightedge and a spirit level to be sure that the tile grid is still running square with the original layout lines.

Pay particular attention to the grout lines as you work. Unlike tiles you lay on floors and counters, wall tiles can sometimes sag on the adhesive and close up the grout seams. You can solve this problem by starting the field on a row of temporary nails or a batten, and supporting each new course with spacers.

When the main field is finished, cut and add edge pieces as needed. Allow the tile adhesive to set according to manufacturer's directions. Then you can come back and install the grout. **11.**

When you frame custom enclosures, plan seats, inset shelves, and other features to accommodate full tiles.

Installing Accessories

Many fiberglass and acrylic showers are manufactured with recessed soap dishes, grab bars, and small corner seats already molded in. In a custom-tiled shower, of course, you have to install these features yourself.

Soap Dishes & Grab Bars

There are two ways to handle these fixtures. One is to tile the wall completely and drill through the tile to surface-mount the accessories with screws. The other, which generally looks better, is to use dish and towel-bar fixtures that match the tile color and grid. Because their mounting areas are multiples of the full tiles, you can add them after you set the field tiles without cutting or trimming.

Note that recessed dishes may require some extra work on the framing and substrate before you start tiling.

You can adhere soap dishes with thinset adhesive applied to the wall and buttered on the back of the dish. For safety, locate dish fixtures where they will not be used as handholds. Grab bars generally require strong fittings that are attached to wall studs behind the tile substrate.

Shower Seats

You can buy prefinished shower seats or forms that you can tile to blend in with the enclosure. These have a seat frame that you mount on the supporting studs. Then you add adhesive, tile, and grout the way you do on the walls. (See "Making a Shower Seat," pages 148 to 149.)

Installing a Soap Dish

Tools and Materials   Easy

- Thinset adhesive
- Small notched trowel
- Pointing trowel
- Masking tape
- Soap dish

TILE TIP: *Although some soap dishes have a built-in bar (intended for a washcloth), they are not designed to withstand the weight of a person. It's wise to use dishes without a bar.*

1 Scrape off any dried adhesive residue from the full tiles surrounding the opening, and spread thinset adhesive on the wall.

2 Use a small trowel to butter the back of the soap dish with adhesive. Then press the dish into place and align it with the adjacent tiles.

3 Maintain pressure on the dish as the adhesive sets by applying two long strips of masking tape across the front edge of the dish.

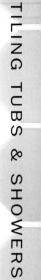

Recessed Soap Dishes

A recessed soap dish is a convenient extra that you can build into your tile job. Some units require a small 2x4 frame to support the bottom and the sides of the dish within the wall. The easiest option is to add a surface-mounted dish. It has a lip that rests on the surrounding tile. You also can add a ceramic dish by making an access hole in the substrate. Use thinset adhesive to fasten a scrap piece of membrane to the inside of the framed support, spread about 1/16 inch of thinset adhesive on the back of the dish, and press it into place.

To mount a recessed soap dish, an extra piece of blocking is needed between studs. Plan for this before you begin installing tile.

Installing a Grab Bar

Tools and Materials — Easy

- Power drill and masonry bit
- Anchors and screws
- Level
- Masking tape
- Screwdriver
- Grab bar

TILE TIP: *For maximum safety, don't rely on anchors in drywall or backer board. Fasten bar mounts directly to wall studs.*

1 *Locate wall studs, generally 16 in. on center. Apply masking tape to the surface of the tile, and drill using a masonry or glass-cutting bit.*

2 *You may not be able to hit a stud with every fastener. In such cases use heavy-duty hollow-wall anchors or toggle bolts.*

3 *Tighten all fasteners until the bar does not move when force is applied to it. Be careful not to overtighten the screws and crack the tile.*

Making a Shower Seat

Tools and Material — *Moderate*

- Measuring tape and masking tape
- Power drill and masonry bit
- Anchors and screws
- Seat form and mortar mix
- Thinset adhesive and trowels
- Sponge float
- Caulking gun

TILE TIP: *For maximum strength, fasten the seat directly into wall studs where possible.*

1 Apply tape over the areas where you will need to attach the seat form. Then measure up from the shower pan to mark the attachment points.

4 Secure the hollow seat form with screws in the anchors. On new construction, you can add nailers between studs and drive screws without anchors.

5 Mix a batch of cement mortar to fill in the seat form. To provide a firm base without air pockets, use a trowel to work the mix into all corners.

8 To avoid a grout seam along the seat edge, use tiles with a bullnose edge on top. The bullnose edges should cover the tiles on the seat face.

9 Set full tiles on the face of the seat, a contrasting color, in this case. To keep them from sagging, you can add tape that laps onto the seat top.

2 *Use a masonry bit in your drill to make holes for screw anchors. The tape helps to prevent chipping on the tile surface glaze.*

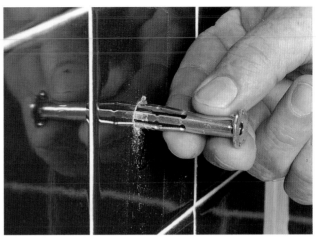

3 *Remove the tape, and insert hollow-wall anchors into the holes. Match the drill bit diameter to the anchors so that they fit snugly.*

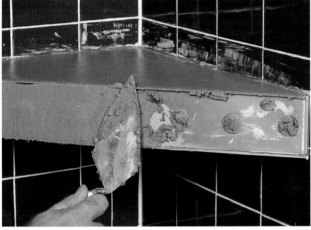

6 *Prepare a sound base for the tile by smoothing out the mortar on the surface of the seat and spreading a thin layer on the front edge.*

7 *Once the mortar is dry, you can apply tile adhesive to the top and front of the seat. Cover the seat completely before raking out ribs of adhesive.*

10 *Use a sponge float to spread grout over the seat top and face. Work the mix back and forth at an angle to fill the seams.*

11 *Instead of grouting the seams along the walls, fill them with a flexible silicone caulking that can withstand slight flexing without cracking.*

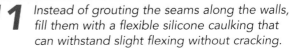

Framing & Tiling Tubs

The easiest way to make a raised tub enclosure is to buy a drop-in tub and frame the platform around it. Tubs with a self-rimming lip overlap tiles on the top of the platform, which eliminates complicated and leak-prone joints between the platform tile and the tub.

Floor Framing Support

In most cases you can rest the tub on the floor and build several steps into the side of your platform. Suspending a tub above the floor is possible but impractical and generally not necessary. For example, with tubs and whirlpool spas about 18 inches deep, you can build three steps, each with a comfortable 6-inch rise. Raise the tub much higher, and you start to have headroom problems in houses with 8-foot ceilings.

Because of the extra weight, however, it's wise to increase the strength of the floor. (Always check manufacturers' recommendations and local building codes, including requirements for approved grab bars or railings.) You can double up existing joists or add new joists spaced closer together than the standard layout of 16 inches on center. Also plan on covering the existing subfloor with ¾-inch exterior-grade plywood, glued and screwed in place. Many acrylic and fiberglass tubs have reinforcing ribs built into the base. But to make the most secure installation and guard against cracking the base finish, many professional installers set the tub base in a supporting bed of quick-setting plaster.

Platform Framing

When you plan the platform and steps, allow for structural framing, such as 2×6s, plus ¾-inch plywood topped with a layer of ½-inch cement-based backer board. Use slip-resistant tiles. On custom projects like this, it's wise to build the platform to suit the tile grid so that you can use full tiles.

When framing, you must allow for supply and drain lines, of course. It's also a good idea to include some kind of access panel or removable section so that you can reach the plumbing lines and make repairs without destroying most of the platform.

Bear in mind that the platform should be at least as rigid as the floor. You may need to use pressure-treated joists set every 12 inches with joists hangers and corner hardware at the joints. Use screws instead of nails for more holding power.

Thinset Tub Enclosure

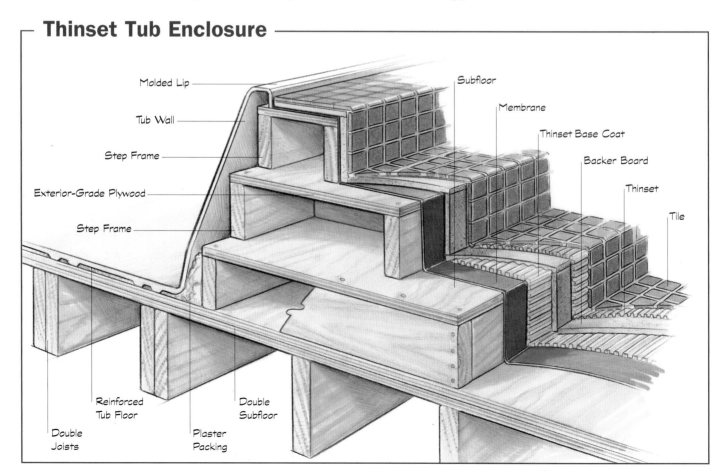

Molded Lip
Tub Wall
Step Frame
Exterior-Grade Plywood
Step Frame
Subfloor
Membrane
Thinset Base Coat
Backer Board
Thinset
Tile
Double Joists
Reinforced Tub Floor
Plaster Packing
Double Subfloor

Tiling the Platform

The layout for a tile platform combines the basic principles used for tiling walls and countertops. Any cut tiles should be more than a half-tile wide, if possible. Be sure to include the width of grout joints when you establish the working lines. A layout stick will help you determine exact locations for the tiles.

Once you have planned the layout for the best tile arrangement and established your working lines, tile the surfaces in the following order: step risers, step treads, platform surface, platform sides, and finally the walls surrounding the platform.

Bear in mind that if the tub is dropped in first, you will need to rout a rabbet around the edges of the tub cutout so that the rim sits flush with the rough platform surface. Then you'll need to tile over the rim with bullnose or quarter-round trim tiles. If the first course of field tiles around the trim tiles needs to be cut, the cut edges will be visible. Also, oval tubs and those with large radiused corners will require complicated cuts and irregularly shaped grout joints. Given these possible complications, consider a self-rimming tub with a raised lip that rests on top of the platform tiles.

If you are using cove trim tiles where the tub platform meets the walls, install these pieces before you set the full tiles on either surface. You might also use coves at the bottom of each riser, but this requires careful planning when you frame the steps. Typically, you finish the front edge of the step treads with bullnose tiles. You also can use special stair-nosing tiles for this purpose, if they are available.

Forming Custom Tubs

Tiled tubs can be virtually any shape or size you want. You can make square-edged enclosures or construct curved, free-form tubs covered with small ceramic mosaic tiles. But building such a tub is very difficult and best left to professionals.

The preferred method for building a tiled tub is to pour a reinforced concrete shell. A waterproof membrane is applied over the concrete shell, followed by a thickset mortar bed. Such a concrete tank requires a strong concrete footing set directly into the ground or exceptional framing that may need steel beams to provide enough strength. Also, the shell must be waterproof, and the floor should slope slightly toward the drain.

Another approach is to build a wooden form and apply a reinforced mortar bed over it. Such installations must be well reinforced, or movement in the wood substructure will crack the mortar bed and tile, causing leaks.

Thickset Tiled Tub

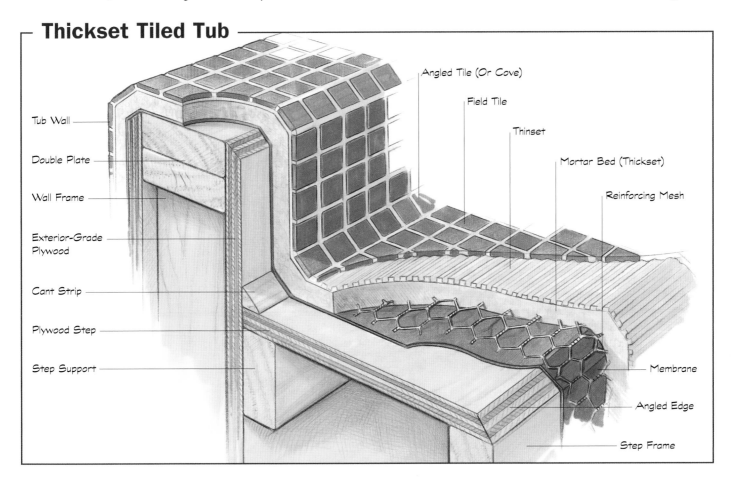

Tub Wall

Double Plate

Wall Frame

Exterior-Grade Plywood

Cant Strip

Plywood Step

Step Support

Angled Tile (Or Cove)

Field Tile

Thinset

Mortar Bed (Thickset)

Reinforcing Mesh

Membrane

Angled Edge

Step Frame

DESIGN IDEAS: TUBS & SHOWERS

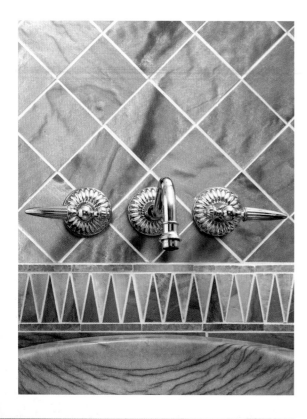

Distinctive border tile, *above left, frames a tile wall.*

Stone tiles, *left, cover a built-in tub surround.*

A mosaic panel, *above, unifies floor and tub tile treatment.*

Natural stone, *opposite, creates a distinctive walk-in shower.*

DESIGN IDEAS: TUBS & SHOWERS

Large tiles, *opposite, match the scale of the high ceilings in this bathroom.*

White wall tiles, *above, are installed in a running-bond pattern.*

A simple color scheme, *below, helps these different shaped tiles work together.*

Accent tiles, *top right, add distinction to the wall of this walk-in shower.*

The rustic charm *of this log home, bottom right, is accentuated by the bright-blue tiles.*

CHAPTER 7

■ ■ ■

INDOOR PROJECTS

Although the most common tile projects are floors, walls, and countertops, there are many other areas around the house where tile can provide an attractive surface that offers more durability and easier maintenance than many building materials. Some of the most popular are fireplace hearths and facings, woodstove surrounds, range hoods, and stairs.

The basics don't change just because the tile is behind a stove or above a kitchen range. But some of these more unusual installations, such as a range hood, can be more challenging because you need to build a solid tile support system. No matter where you install tile, it pays to remember the basics of preparation. On structures without tile where you normally might use furring strips and ½-inch drywall, you should consider a beefier design of 2x4s and cement-based backer board.

Also bear in mind that when you tile near any combustion source, such as a fireplace or woodstove, you should first check local building codes (and tile material data sheets) to be sure you are using fire-safe methods and materials.

Fireplaces

Whether you are building a new fireplace or remodeling an existing unit, you can use ceramic tile to make an elegant, fire-safe covering for the hearth and fireplace face wall. You can tile the hearth only, the hearth and firebox surround, or add a single row of decorative tiles around the fireplace opening as an accent. In all cases, check local building codes, and be sure that you make a fire-safe installation.

Selecting Materials

Around a fireplace, use tile that is resistant to both heat and the impact of an accidentally dropped log. Heavy-duty quarry tiles, pavers, or glazed floor tiles are all good choices. If the manufacturer offers more than one thickness, go with the beefier size. If you are tiling over concrete, brick, or other masonry, use nonflammable heat-resistant mortar, such as a dry-set cement. Do not use organic mastics. If you are tiling over an existing wood floor, it's wise to install at least one layer of cement-based backer board. Remember that on installations that extend an existing hearth or add a new one, you may need to strengthen the subfloor.

Hearth Design

The hearth on the floor in front of a fireplace should be covered with tile, brick, or other masonry material that can stand up to sparks and embers. You can cut the masonry area out of the finished floor to make a tiled hearth flush with the surrounding floor. But it's easier to leave the existing wood in place and create a slightly raised hearth by applying backer board and trimming the edges. **1–2.** It generally looks best to extend the hearth at least a tile or two on each side of the opening. Typically, the hearth rests on a full foundation or a poured concrete slab about 4 inches thick supported by extra framing and hardware. The hearth generally extends at least 16 inches out and 8 inches on each side of the firebox. If the existing hearth isn't up to code, it's a good idea to bring it up to code before tiling.

Face-Wall Design

On masonry fireplaces, you can set tiles in a bed of mortar spread over lath attached to the existing brick, block, or stone. With prefab metal fireplaces, you should be able to build a surround to suit the tile grid and cover the framed enclosure with cement-based backer board. Use a heat-resistant epoxy mortar to apply tile to metal and a heat-resistant cement mortar on masonry surfaces.

Setting the Tiles

You can set ceramic tile over an existing masonry hearth if the surface is relatively flat. Rigidity is usually not a problem with masonry. If you are dealing with a rough surface, a thick bond coat of mortar will fill mortar joints and provide a suitable surface for the tile. Grind down any high spots, and clean the surface thoroughly to remove soot or dirt. Then apply a bond coat to fill in irregularities. When the bond coat dries, make your layout lines, and apply a second coat of mortar to set the tiles according to the manufacturer's instructions. **3–4.**

To tile either a flush or raised hearth, start by tiling the front with full tiles. It pays to make a test fit in advance, accounting for tile and grout joints. After the tiles have set up, grout the joints, and if the hearth is raised, add trim. **5.** Caulk the seam between the tile and trim and between the wall and the hearth.

Tile provides a safe fireplace surround and hearth even where most of the walls are paneled with wood.

Tiling a Hearth

Tools and Materials — *Moderate*

- Chalk-line box
- Thinset and notched trowel
- Cement-based backer board
- Power drill and screws
- Rafter square

TILE TIP: *To strengthen a floor without adding double layers of plywood or backer board, which will raise the hearth, you can double up the supporting joists.*

1 Locate the midpoint of the opening, and mark a line to center the hearth. Generally, hearths should be at least 16 in. deep.

2 Score and snap a sheet of backer board, and set it in a bed of thinset mortar. Leave a gap for caulking next to the fireplace, and secure with screws.

3 Snap layout lines for your tile, and rake out a bed of thinset over the backer board with the notched edge of your trowel.

4 On a hearth you may want to start with a dry layout to be sure the tiles will fit. Embed the cut tiles first, and follow with full tiles and edging.

5 Add trim around the edges of the hearth. Wood strips with mitered corners make a nice transition between a wood floor and a tiled hearth.

Tiling a Face Wall

There is no one correct way to tile the face of a fireplace, because there are so many different types of installations. Over rough brick, for example, you might need to add layers of metal lath and mortar to create a smooth setting bed. Over a zero-clearance prefab unit with walls that never get very hot, you might frame-in the face and install a layer of cement-based backer board.

Generally you can follow the same approach as you do tiling walls. The main difference, of course, is that most installations require heat-resistant materials such as epoxy-based mortar to apply tile to metal, and cement-based mortar over masonry surfaces or backer board. Be sure you check the installation against local codes, which are strict when it comes to fire safety.

A common stumbling block on wall installations (and fireplaces, too) is keeping tiles from sagging until they set. One solution is to install a row of temporary support nails or a wooden batten along the top of where you'll set the bottom row. (See pages 103 and 143.) Once the main tiles have set, you can remove the support and secure the bottom row of tiles by taping them to the set tiles above. Another option is to build a temporary wood trestle to bridge the opening and support the tiles.

On many prefab units, you can bring the tile right to the built-in lip around the fireplace opening. On masonry fireplaces, you need to trim the edge with bullnose tile or decorative tile strips. Be sure to make a test layout starting with full tiles around the opening so you can see where partial tiles may be needed.

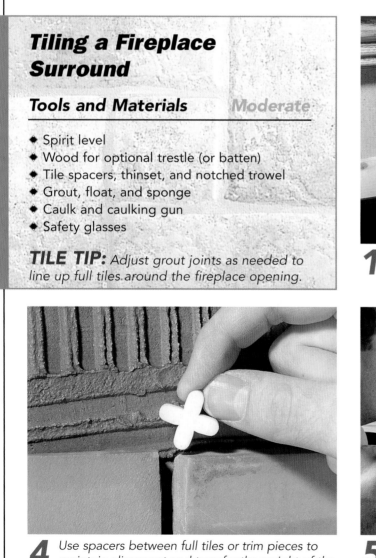

Tiling a Fireplace Surround

Tools and Materials   *Moderate*

- Spirit level
- Wood for optional trestle (or batten)
- Tile spacers, thinset, and notched trowel
- Grout, float, and sponge
- Caulk and caulking gun
- Safety glasses

TILE TIP: *Adjust grout joints as needed to line up full tiles around the fireplace opening.*

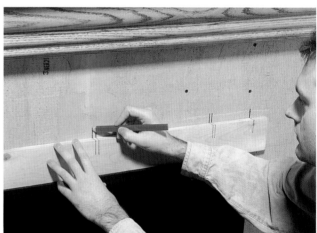

1 *Use a layout stick to plan the installation and prepare for a test fit. Be sure to size cut tiles on each side of the opening so that they match.*

4 *Use spacers between full tiles or trim pieces to maintain alignment and transfer the weight of the tiles down to the lip or trestle.*

5 *Once the tile is securely set, generally overnight, use a float to grout the joints. Clean off the dried grout haze using a damp sponge.*

A variety of tile shapes *combine to trim an unusual-shaped opening and provide the intricate appearance normally associated with a carved wooden surround.*

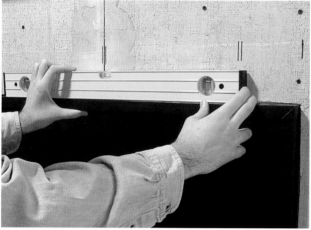

2 *Check for level across the fireplace lip (on a prefab unit) or the lintel across a masonry opening. Adjust the grout joint to keep the tiles level.*

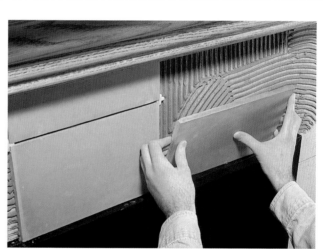

3 *Use a notched trowel to rake out a bed of thinset adhesive over the substrate, and set full tiles (or trim strip tiles) around the fireplace opening.*

6 *Use wood or tile trim to make the transition from the tile to the wall. Check local codes for clearances from the fireplace opening to the wood trim.*

7 *Install a bead of flexible grout to prevent cracking in the seam between the tiles on the face wall and the tiles on the hearth.*

Woodstoves

Ceramic tile is a good choice for hearths and walls around woodstoves because it can withstand heat and sparks without shrinking, cracking, or charring the way wood does. But as always, where fire safety is concerned, you should check local codes to be sure that your tile installation is fire-safe.

Basic Safety Considerations

There are several basic guidelines about placing combustible materials near a fire source, but the exact rules can vary from one jurisdiction to another. Safety clearances can also vary depending on the type of materials you have on the floor and wall—and on the type of stove you install. For example, stoves with a heat shield attached to the back generally can be much closer to walls than stoves without shields.

If you're installing a new stove, you almost certainly will need a building permit. The job can require structural alterations and an inspection even if you use prefab metal chimney sections. If you're tiling an existing installation, it's wise to be sure that the old stove and flue are up to code (and clean) as part of the project.

Reducing Clearances to Tile

You can make a safe installation by keeping a stove 3 feet or more from the nearest wall. But most people don't want a stove sticking into the middle of a room. To prevent that, you can buy a stove with a heat-dissipating design. You can also make a tile installation on a false wall that creates an air baffle against the main house wall. With the right combination, you should be able to set a stove only 12 inches away from the wall.

Beneath the stove you normally have to install at least one layer of cement-based backer board. Walls often are more critical because stoves are designed to throw most of their heat through the sides and top. To cope with the heat, the most efficient wall consists of ½-inch noncombustible insulation board or 24-gauge sheet metal set 1 inch away from the house wall on noncombustible spacers. Most jurisdictions allow you to substitute backer board (a standard tile substrate) for the insulation board, but you should check to be sure.

Once you decide on the best type of code-approved installation, you can plan the tile layout and select trim tiles. Bear in mind that you may need a radius trim to conceal the thickness of your substrate. You can use wood trim farther away from the stove.

Typical Clearances

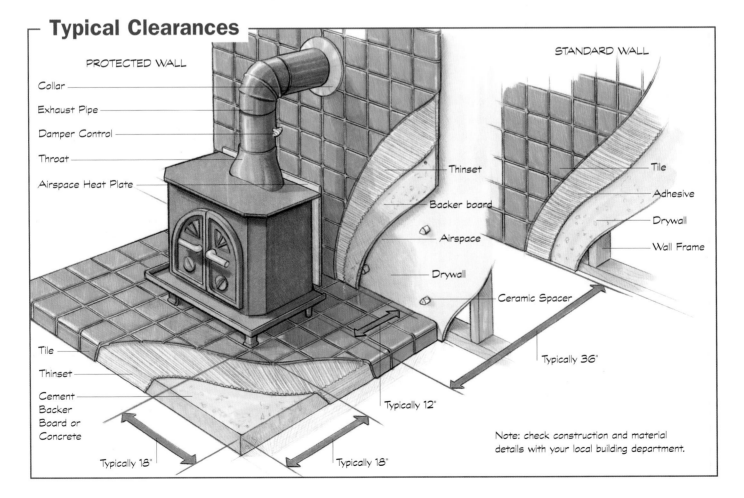

PROTECTED WALL

Collar
Exhaust Pipe
Damper Control
Throat
Airspace Heat Plate

Tile
Thinset
Cement Backer Board or Concrete

Typically 18"   Typically 18"

Thinset
Backer board
Airspace
Drywall
Ceramic Spacer

Typically 12"

STANDARD WALL

Tile
Adhesive
Drywall
Wall Frame

Typically 36"

Note: check construction and material details with your local building department.

Tiling a Spaced Woodstove Surround

Tools and Materials   *Moderate*

- Spacers and fasteners
- Variable-speed drill
- Cement-based backer board
- Notched trowel and thinset
- Grout tools and materials

TILE TIP: *You can buy kits of ceramic spacers for spaced walls. Don't use wood blocks.*

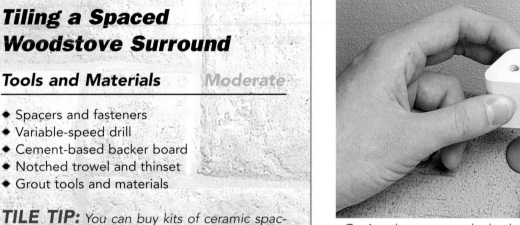

1 Attach spacers to the back of the backer board using thinset. Then use the spacer holes as guides to drill holes through the backer board.

2 Secure the backer board by tightening a fastener that runs through the fireproof spacer into the house wall. The board should stand off 1 in.

3 Use a notched trowel to spread thinset over the backer board. The bed should be thick enough to bury the fastener and washer.

4 Set the main tiles in the pattern of your choice. Then trim the tiles that will surround the vent pipe using tile nippers.

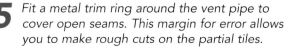

5 Fit a metal trim ring around the vent pipe to cover open seams. This margin for error allows you to make rough cuts on the partial tiles.

Range Hoods

You can buy a range hood to tile or build a custom hood. But building one from scratch is quite a project for do-it-yourselfers because it's really several projects in one. You need to fabricate the hood structure and build-in wiring, a fan, a grease filter, a duct, and an exterior vent. It's often easier to add tile to a factory-made hood. Bear in mind, though, that many standard hoods made with thin sheet metal are not rigid enough to support tile.

Range-Hood Materials

Stove fires are among the most common types of house fires. They can start so easily and spread so rapidly that you should take care not to build a hood out of combustible materials that could add fuel to a blaze.

You may find that a building inspector will allow you to make a hood with wood framing as long as both sides are covered with fire-rated drywall. Or you may be able to cover the framing with cement-based backer board, which makes a good substrate for tile. Material selection may also be influenced by how far away from the range you locate the hood.

◆ **Steel Hoods.** A sheet-metal company can fabricate a heavy-gauge steel hood that will support tile. After roughening the steel surface with sandpaper, you set the tiles with an epoxy adhesive or with a latex-cement thinset mortar with additives that bond to steel. Some are rated to resist temperatures over 300°F, which is a lot hotter than a range hood will get during normal operation.

◆ **Wooden Hoods.** You can build a plywood-covered wood frame and install drywall or backer board over the structure. If codes permit, this may be the best choice if you have an unusual installation or plan to use an unusual combination of tile sizes.

◆ **Prefab Hoods.** The thin sheet metal generally used for these hoods is too flexible to support the weight of the tile without cracking the grout joints.

Hood Tile

Where the tiles are concerned, you don't need extra thickness for impact resistance the way you do on a fireplace hearth. In fact, because of weight, thin glazed ceramic wall tiles are preferable. If the hood is curved, you can use ceramic-mosaic sheets.

Hood Dimensions

On a custom hood, plan ahead to avoid a lot of partial tiles and angled cuts. For example, you can design the hood apron to match the size of full tiles plus a grout

You can use full tiles on an apron, and make angle cuts (allowing for grout joints or trim) on the sloping surfaces.

joint. However, most range hoods slope inward from bottom to top, which means you'll have to use some wedge-shaped tiles.

Tiling a Hood

There are so many different range-hood designs that there is no one way to install the tile. But you should have good results following basic rules, such as using full tiles in a symmetrical pattern centered in the most visible area. If you need partial tiles (aside from angled tiles on the sloping edges), place them along the wall.

Apply adhesive according to the manufacturer's instructions with a notched trowel. You'll probably need to support the first row of tiles with a batten to prevent sagging. On hoods with finished edges below eye level, you can often trim the edge with bullnose tile. On higher installations and hoods with a thick edge, you should select tile that comes with matching radius-edge or other trim to conceal the substrate. Let the adhesive cure overnight before grouting, and let the grout cure overnight before putting the hood into service.

Tiling a Range Hood

Tools and Materials   Challenging

- Cement-based backer board
- Variable-speed drill and fasteners
- Notched trowel and thinset
- Wood (and wood sealer) or tile trim
- Tile cutter and wood trim tools
- Grout materials

TILE TIP: *Fasten wood trim to the plywood for the best bond, allowing for the thickness of backer board, thinset, and tile to come.*

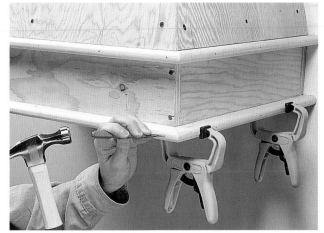

1 *Frame the apron with hardwood trim applied with glue and finishing nails. You can also use tile trim over cement-based backer board.*

2 *Once the wood trim is secured you can apply panels of cement-based backer board to the apron and sloping faces of the hood above.*

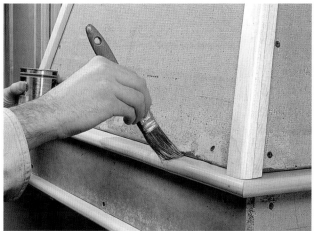

3 *To protect the wood trim as you tile, apply a protective coat of sealer. This makes it easier to wipe away traces of thinset and grout.*

4 *A series of mosaic-like tiles are used on this project to focus attention on the apron. No spacers are needed because the tiles have spacer lugs.*

5 *Set full tiles in a ribbed bed of thinset on each sloping face of the hood. Where the fields meet, you can use wood trim, tile trim, or a grout joint.*

Stairs

It is possible to tile both stair treads—the part you step on—and stair risers—the vertical panel between treads. But it can be difficult for do-it-yourselfers to match the design of wood steps and create an overhang at each tread. The more doable and often better looking project is to use tile on the risers only as a decorative feature, and stick with traditional wood planks with an overhang on the treads.

If you want to tile the treads, consider ordering special stair-tread tiles that come with a rounded nosing to project slightly past the front edge of the riser. Without getting too technical about it, this design does make a safer step that's easier to negotiate than a right-angle box shape with no overhang.

Another option is to use large, unglazed quarry or paver tiles that are often used for the treads on outdoor steps. You may be able to create a small tread overhang with tile and supporting trim strips. You can't project a standard floor tile past the riser without support because it is too likely to crack.

Whatever tile you select for the treads should be slip-resistant and durable enough to withstand heavy foot traffic. Tiles for risers, on the other hand, can be relatively thin glazed wall tiles. You can install them in a continuous band across the riser or add just one accent tile in the center of the riser.

Design Considerations

Most stairs are strong enough to support tile because they are designed to support people. But some treads do flex slightly, which is just enough to disrupt tile grout and lead to repair problems and possible safety hazards. It's difficult to detect minimal flexing, although the sound of squeaking wood is a sure sign that stair components are moving. On an existing staircase with this problem, you can take several approaches.

The most drastic improvement is to add a center stringer. This effectively cuts the span of each tread and riser in half, providing twice as much support. But you can also screw steel angle brackets to treads and risers, insert wooden wedges, and add long wood screws to create a more secure connection between the stairs and supporting walls. Another option is to install wooden blocks with glue and screws along the seams between treads and risers at midspan where they are weakest and most likely to flex.

Of course, it's possible to make these improvements only if you have access from below to the stair framing or if you remove a tread. But if you are planning to cover treads and risers with tile, you can drive screws through exposed surfaces to tighten up the structure. If you do this, it's wise to countersink the holes so that screwheads are flush and cannot crack the tiles.

If you are tiling over concrete steps (a project that is more likely outside than inside), clean the masonry surfaces to improve adhesion, and repair any cracks or other faults that could create weak spots under the tile. If you are building a new set of wooden steps for tiling, provide a suitable substrate such as exterior-grade ¾-inch plywood. On deep treads you can use two layers of the plywood to prevent flexing as long as you stay within code limits for riser and tread dimensions. You can also guard against cracking by using a flexible caulk along the seam between tread tiles and riser tiles.

You can combine heavy-duty tread tiles *that have a built-in nosing with thinner, more decorative tiles on the risers.*

Tiling Stairs

Tools and Materials · *Moderate*

- Screwdriver and fasteners
- Hardware, or wood blocks and glue
- Sander and medium-grit sandpaper
- Trowel and adhesive
- Caulk and caulking gun

TILE TIP: *Set riser tiles on temporary spacers or nails to keep them from sagging and closing up the caulk joints at the treads.*

1 You can strengthen stairs with closed framing by driving screws at an angle through the face of the riser and into the tread.

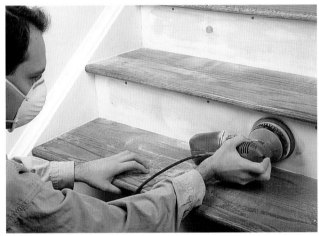

2 To improve the adhesive bond on risers, scrape off old paint, and sand down any rough spots with medium-grit paper.

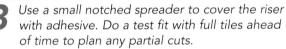

3 Use a small notched spreader to cover the riser with adhesive. Do a test fit with full tiles ahead of time to plan any partial cuts.

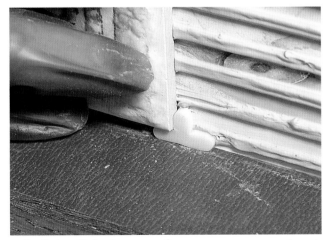

4 Snip off the bottom of a spacer so you can insert it between the tile and the tread. You can also use finishing nails to keep the tile from sagging.

5 Once the tile has set, grout the vertical seams, and wipe away the final grout haze. Use flexible caulk in the tread seams.

DESIGN IDEAS: INDOOR PROJECTS

An exhaust-hood border, above, ties the area into the rest of the design.

A large fireplace area, below, relies on tile for a cohesive design.

Tiled stair risers, right, add a distinctive touch to this home.

Natural stone tiles, opposite, give an understated look to this fireplace.

DESIGN IDEAS: INDOOR PROJECTS

Terra-cotta tiles, *opposite, complement the cabinetry in this room.*

Unusual shapes, *left, add interest to this fireplace and hearth.*

A tile surround, *above, becomes a focal point in this room.*

Colorful tiles, *below, are used as a surround for a rotisserie.*

CHAPTER 8

•••

OUTDOOR PROJECTS

Ceramic and stone tiles are among the most elegant surfacing materials you can use for a patio, walk, or entryway. They can also be the most expensive.

Unglazed quarry tile and pavers are generally the most popular tiles for outdoor patios and walks. But you can use glazed tiles that provide adequate traction in special circumstances—for instance, when the tiles on an interior floor extend past a sliding glass door onto a connecting patio.

The type of tile you choose may be determined by the weather in your region. In warm, relatively dry regions, for example, soft-bodied, nonvitreous pavers are often used. These include low-fired, handmade Mexican pavers and cement-based saltillo tiles. Both types are porous and will not hold up in wet or cold climates.

In most areas of the country, you will need a hard-bodied vitreous or impervious tile, such as porcelain pavers or vitreous quarry tiles. In cold climates, of course, you need to select tile and grout that resist freezing temperatures.

Tiling Existing Concrete

If you're starting from scratch, you can pour a solid slab to support the tile. If you have a solid slab already, you'll generally need to do only a little cleaning and touch-up work. But you also can use tile to cover up surface cracks and other problems in an older patio, and let the existing masonry serve as a foundation.

If the slab is badly fractured, you may have to pour new concrete footings and refinish the surface. It's a lot of work, but it makes sense when compared with paying someone to break up the old patio and cart it away.

If the slab is covered with surface cracks but is still flat and stable, it is a good candidate for pouring a thin cover slab. If parts of the slab are tilting in different directions and bobbing up and down each season like slow-motion icebergs, you will have to beef up the slab support system. It's wise to consult an engineer or experienced masonry contractor about this work.

You can't expect good results patching major cracks on a slab that moves seasonally. The cracks will open again and disrupt the tile surface.

Testing the Surface

Before you clean the surface and make repairs, it's a good idea to test the concrete to see whether a curing agent was used. Some of these agents can interfere with the adhesive bond between the slab and the tile. Some surface sealers can have the same effect.

To make the test, sprinkle some water on the slab and see if it beads up or soaks in. If the water beads up, a curing agent was probably used.

To prevent a curing agent or sealer from disrupting the tile bond, you can sandblast the surface. The homeowner equivalent is pressure-washing. But you have to handle these machines with caution because a high-pressure stream of water can be strong enough to pit solid concrete. You don't generally need to use chemical removers with a high-pressure spray.

Preparing the Surface

Start by grinding down any high spots with a power grinder. **1.** To fix small cracks and chips, start by digging out the crevices with a narrow cold chisel or screwdriver. Be sure to remove any loose mortar. It's also a good idea to use a stiff brush or compressed air to clean cracks of any dirt, old leaves, or other debris. **2.**

You can use a mason's trowel to fill cracks and holes with masonry patching compound. **3.** You may also need to fill low spots with the patching compound.

If you don't pressure-wash, you can use a commercial concrete cleaner to remove any grease, wax, or other

Large tiles make a handsome patio that will not rot, splinter, or provide a food source for termites.

contaminants. **4.** Rinse thoroughly with water, and let the slab dry. **5.**

To prevent puddling, slope the slab slightly away from the house. You can test this easily enough by checking the slab after a heavy rain or by spraying the slab with a hose.

To correct the problem before tiling, you need to coat a thick bed of cement mortar over the entire patio, sloping it about ⅛ inch per foot. After the mortar cures, you can set the tile with thinset mortar.

Preparing an Existing Concrete Surface

Tools and Materials   Easy

- Power grinder (or hammer and cold chisel)
- Broom and mop
- Patching mortar and mason's trowel
- Hose and straightedge
- Scrub brush and detergent

TILE TIP: Pressure-washing often can remove debris from cracks, clear loose mortar, and clean the surface in one operation.

1 Check for high spots by moving a straightedge across the slab. Then use a power grinder with an abrasive wheel to reduce the high spots.

2 Sweep away dirt and debris, which can interfere with tile adhesion. Pressure-washing or a blast of compressed air works well on cracks.

3 Clear loose concrete and debris from cracks. Then use a trowel to press in patching mortar. Make several passes to be sure the crack is filled.

4 To improve the bond between the slab and the tile, clean the slab with a pressure-washer—or do it the old-fashioned way, by hand.

5 Use a garden hose to rinse the surface thoroughly and remove any traces of cleaning agents, which could interfere with the adhesive bond.

Building a New Concrete Base

To build a tiled patio or walk, you'll need to start with a solid concrete slab. To build one, you'll probably need a permit and a plan that shows its location and construction details. You can check the requirements with the local building department.

Basic Slab Design

A typical slab has several layers that combine to strengthen the concrete. To reduce stress, they should rest on undisturbed or compacted soil. This helps to prevent settling that can cause cracks. In cold regions you generally have to build a perimeter foundation for the slab that extends below the frost line. That may require extra excavation and other work that may be beyond the capabilities of do-it-yourselfers.

The bottom layer of a sturdy, code-approved slab usually consists of several inches of compacted gravel. You pour the concrete on top of it. To strengthen the pour, you need to embed a layer of welded wire. This is the home version of large-scale rebars that you see set into highway bridges and other commercial concrete structures. To provide maximum strength, try to set the flattened welded wire (it comes in a roll) in the bottom third of the pour. To do this, you can use pieces of brick or specialty supports called chairs to suspend the wire as you pour the concrete.

In yards where you have drainage problems or loose, sandy soil, you may need to take other measures to be sure that a slab is solidly installed. Be sure to check the specific building practices required by local codes.

On large slabs, you'll also need one or more control joints. These slices in the slab surface (you see them every few feet in concrete sidewalks) control minor cracking.

If the patio joins the house, you'll also need an isolation joint so that the structures don't work against each other. To make one before pouring the concrete, temporarily insert a strip of wood to create about a 3/8-inch gap between the concrete and the foundation. When the pour sets, fill the space with backer rod and caulk.

Lastly, plan the slab to account for even multiples of the tiles you plan to use. Also account for the grout joints. If you're building from scratch, you can eliminate the need for partial tiles.

Patio Slab Construction

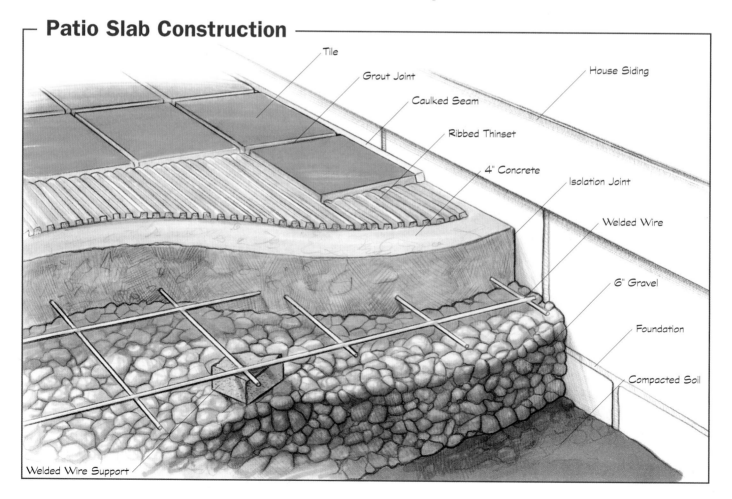

Tile
Grout Joint
Caulked Seam
Ribbed Thinset
4" Concrete
House Siding
Isolation Joint
Welded Wire
6" Gravel
Foundation
Compacted Soil
Welded Wire Support

Tile Tip — Cutting a Control Joint

It may seem strange to slice up the surface of a slab and cut what amounts to big, straight cracks on purpose. But each shallow groove acts as a kind of magnet that collects minor cracking where you can't see it. You can cut these joints with a masonry saw after the concrete hardens or use a jointing trowel against a straightedge guide while the mix is still wet.

Cut control joints *using a masonry blade once the concrete hardens. You can also cut them in wet concrete with a special trowel.*

▲ **In a large outdoor space,** *you can use contrasting tile colors to define separate areas.*

▶ **In small outdoor spaces,** *use one size and color of tile to make the area seem larger.*

Excavating the Site

Once the batter boards are up and you have the patio area marked out, use a sharply edged shovel to cut through the sod. **1.** If you slice through the ground to create manageable strips a few feet wide, you can undercut the roots, roll up the turf, and use it elsewhere.

In any case, you need to remove enough soil to make way for the slab and its foundation. Also remember to excavate enough dirt around the edges to allow room for the form boards and stakes. As for the depth, you generally need to make room for about 6 inches of gravel and another 4 inches for concrete.

Remember that you need solid ground beneath the slab. If you dig too deeply and leave a lot of loose dirt in place, it will compact under the weight of the concrete, which can cause cracking. You can prevent this problem by digging down uniformly to a set level. But because that's difficult to do without a bulldozer or a backhoe, you'll probably have to use a tamper or vibrating compactor to firm up a few spots. You can rent a compactor for the project.

Forming the Slab

Next come the forms. To set them up squarely, follow your layout strings set up on the batter boards. Double-check for square by measuring the diagonals of the slab, which should be equal. It's also important to check the boards with a level to make sure that they have a consistent slope. **2–3.** Once the boards (typically 2×6s) are screwed to the supporting stakes, take the time to back-

---

Making Forms for Slabs

Tools and Materials   **Easy**

- Wood for batter boards, stakes, and forms
- Shovel and sledgehammer
- Hammer and clamps
- Spirit level, mason's string, and drill
- Snips, welded wire, and wire supports
- Trowel and concrete installation tools
- Concrete

TILE TIP: Keep the slab surface moist for several days to improve hardness as it cures.

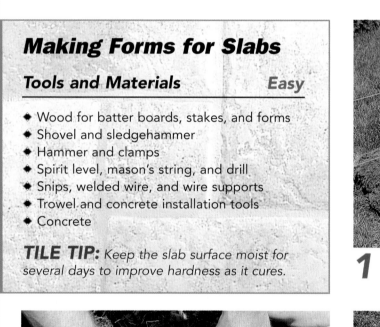

1 Use batter boards set just outside the corners of the patio area to support strings, which guide the excavation and locate the forms.

4 Install a layer of welded wire to reinforce the slab. You can cut the rolled material to size with an electrician's pliers or tin snips.

5 Once the reinforcing wire is cut to size, set it on sections of brick (or specialized supports called chairs) to suspend it in the pour.

fill the forms. Shovel loose dirt against the back of the forms, and tamp the fill in place. This provides extra support for the boards and helps to keep them from shifting when you pour in the concrete.

When the slab area is formed up, you can add the gravel and rake it out to the slight slope you need for drainage. If possible, also compact this layer. You can do this with a roller or a mechanical tamper. Pounding down on soil or gravel with a 2×4 works on small areas, but doing this would take you hours on a slab.

Before you order concrete (mixing enough on your own to make a patio slab isn't sensible), measure and cut the welded-wire reinforcement. Try to position the wire about one-third of the way up from the bottom of the concrete area set on small sections of brick. **4–5.**

Estimating Concrete Orders

Companies that sell ready-mix concrete take orders by the cubic yard. To calculate the space within your forms in their terms, multiply length times width times the average form depth. To estimate a patio slab that is 15 feet long, 10 feet wide, and 4 inches deep, for example, multiply 15 by 10 (150 square feet), and that total by 0.33 (one third of a foot of depth, or 4 inches) to get 50 cubic feet. To convert that figure into cubic yards, divide by 27—about 1.8 cubic yards. On all but small projects, it pays to round up to the next full yard to make sure you have enough material. If you plan to mix your own, remember that one wheelbarrow-size batch makes less than 3 cubic feet. You would need about nine batches to make just 1 cubic yard. (See p. 180 for **6–7** text.)

2 Drive 2x4 stakes with a slanted or V-pointed tip around the outside edge of the excavation. They will support the main form boards.

3 Temporarily clamp the forms against the stakes, and check them with a level. Once you have established the position, screw them in place.

6 Slide a trowel up and down between the form boards and the mix to eliminate voids and firm up the edges of the slab.

7 If you don't have the kind of long-handled float used by contractors, try a long 2x4 straightedge to smooth the concrete surface.

Finishing a Slab

You can have a ready-mix company spread the concrete for you—up to a point. You'll have to shovel the mix into corners, be sure that the welded wire is properly embedded, and use different trowels to cut control joints and finish the edges (Step **6**, p. 179). All in all, pouring a slab is a job that most DIYers would be wise to turn over to a contractor.

The most difficult operation for most people is to smooth out the surface. If you are leveling a narrow patio or walkway, you can use a board wide enough to rest on top of the forms. By working the board back and forth, you can gradually fill in small voids and smooth out the surface as you move along the forms. On a larger surface, you can use a long 2×4 or other straightedge (Step **7**, p. 179). Most pros use a large, lightweight float with a long handle. These are generally available at tool-rental shops. However you smooth the surface, don't overwork the concrete. It brings excess water to the surface and creates uneven distribution of the concrete ingredients.

Before the concrete hardens, you need to cut control joints. You may also want to check into the process of curing, which can be quite complicated. In a nutshell, this is a gradual process of hardening that provides strength and durability. If the concrete dries out too quickly, it can lose strength. If you keep the surface damp for several days, it gains strength. You can do this by misting the surface with a hose several times a day, applying a special sealer that traps moisture, or covering the wet concrete slab with plastic sheeting.

Laying the Tile

Once the concrete is cured (or repaired and cleaned if you're working on an existing slab), snap your working lines on the concrete. You can use the same approach you use for tiling floors. But if you planned ahead to accommodate full tiles in the size of your slab, the layout should be straightforward. **1–3.**

Trowel on the thinset adhesive with a notched trowel matched to the tile and adhesive according to manufacturer's recommendations. On an uneven slab, first you may need to apply a thin bond coat of mortar over the entire surface with a smooth trowel. Remember to check the working temperature limits of the adhesive. **4–7.**

Set the tiles in place, twisting slightly to embed them in the adhesive. As always, check your work frequently with a straightedge to make sure the tiles are level and aligned. Then apply an appropriate grout as recommended by the tile manufacturer. **8.**

Laying the Tiles

Tools and Materials   Moderate

- Measuring tape and chalk-line box
- Thinset and notched trowel
- Tile and spacers
- Grout
- Straightedge

TILE TIP: *Test layouts are essential on jobs with several built-in limitations, for example, the edge of an existing slab and a support post or other structures that interrupt the tile field.*

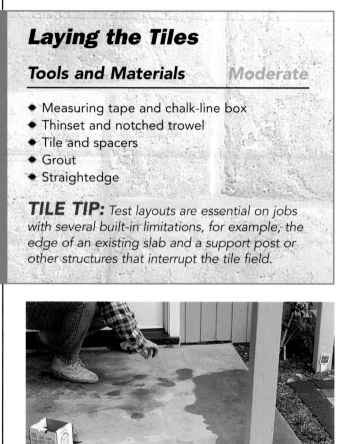

3 Working back from the notched tile that aligns with the edge of the slab, snap chalk lines to guide the full-sized field tiles.

6 If you encounter a low spot, fill it with a slurry of concrete patch material. Generally, it pays to test the slab with a straightedge ahead of time.

1 The support post on this covered entryway controls the layout. You have to make sure that it falls on a seam, not in the middle of a full tile.

2 On a job like this, you may have to experiment with different test layouts. Then you can cut the first notch and move on to the main field.

4 Measure and cut the other side of the post notch. Then trowel on thinset adhesive with a notched trowel. Set spacers at the joints.

5 As you work into the main field, rake out a larger area of thinset, and set full tiles in rows. Measure rows periodically to check for square.

7 You can smooth the patch slurry over a low spot, but a soupy mix is almost self-leveling. Check the manufacturer's specs about hardening time.

8 Apply grout with a sponge-faced trowel or squeegee, working at a diagonal to the joints. Use flexible grout in seams against the house.

Tiling Entry Steps

To tile over a set of concrete steps or a landing, follow the same basic procedures used on patios. But there are a few wrinkles to this project.

First of all, you need to consider safety. That means allowing for a code-approved handrail on steps and staying within approved limits on stair treads and risers. You can check these with the local building department, but generally the rise should be no less than 4 inches and no greater than 7¾ inches. Treads typically must be at least 3 feet wide and about 10 inches deep. If old steps don't meet code, make the necessary improvements. This may include removing an old handrail and installing a new one through the tile. You should also have an isolation joint between the steps and the house foundation so that the two structures don't work against each other.

Tile the Steps

You can use the same tiles on steps that you use on patios. Remember to mention to the supplier that the tiles will be used outside so that you get vitreous tile, which prevents water penetration.

Lay out the steps carefully, particularly if you are tiling both treads and risers. If you are adding tiles to the risers, for example, you need to take their thickness into account when you plan the treads. Generally, the riser tile thickness is covered with a bullnose tile on the tread. Plan on making a test layout.

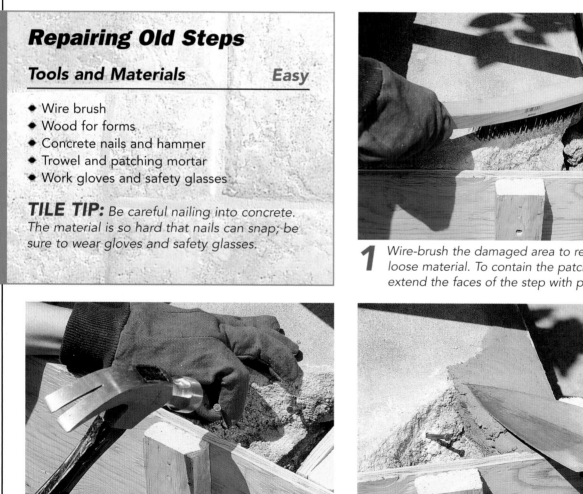

Repairing Old Steps

Tools and Materials   Easy

- Wire brush
- Wood for forms
- Concrete nails and hammer
- Trowel and patching mortar
- Work gloves and safety glasses

TILE TIP: *Be careful nailing into concrete. The material is so hard that nails can snap; be sure to wear gloves and safety glasses.*

1 Wire-brush the damaged area to remove any loose material. To contain the patch material, extend the faces of the step with plywood.

2 To help the patch adhere, you can coat the step with a concrete bonding agent. It also helps to set a few concrete nails about halfway in.

3 Trowel on fresh patching mortar to fill up the cavity. Work the trowel along the insides of the forms to create smooth edges without voids.

Tiling a Pool Deck

To start with, it's wise to confine your efforts to the deck area and let a pool contractor do any tile work in the pool. On concrete pools it's also a good idea to let the contractor install the preformed coping, or edging. Outside those round-edge sections, you can go to town with borders and patterns of tile basically the same way you would on a patio.

But no matter what type of in-ground pool you have, you can install an isolation joint and tile to its structural boundary. Start by compacting the dirt adjacent to the pool coping. Consider renting a mechanical tamper (a heavy machine that vibrates to solidify soil) and compacting loose fill around a new pool.

Follow up with standard slab construction, including a base of 6 inches of gravel and 4 inches of poured concrete reinforced with welded wire. When you build forms for the pool-surround, build in the same kind of slope (about ¼ inch or so per linear foot) that's used on patios. Slope the surround away from the pool on all sides. Locate the outer perimeter of the surround a few inches above grade to prevent water-washed soil and other contaminants from flowing into the pool.

Contrasting tiles help to define boundaries that make the area around a pool more attractive and safe.

Pool Deck Construction

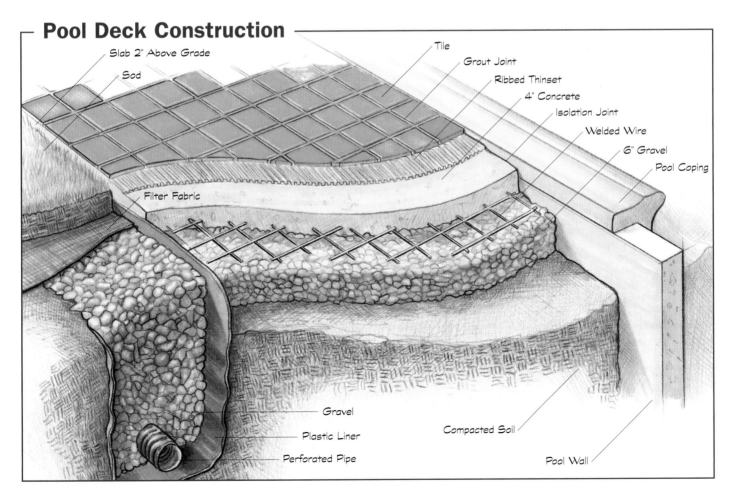

Slab 2" Above Grade

Sod

Filter Fabric

Tile

Grout Joint

Ribbed Thinset

4" Concrete

Isolation Joint

Welded Wire

6" Gravel

Pool Coping

Gravel

Plastic Liner

Perforated Pipe

Compacted Soil

Pool Wall

DESIGN IDEAS: OUTDOOR PROJECTS

Terra-cotta pavers, opposite, are a favorite floor covering for outdoor living areas.

Porcelain tiles, above, are a good choice for pool and fountain decoration.

Colorful tiles, below, draw attention to this small water garden.

A **combination** of natural stone and tile, top right, creates a distinctive garden fountain.

Tiled steps, bottom right, call attention to this curving outdoor stairway.

DESIGN IDEAS: OUTDOOR PROJECTS

Marble tiles, opposite, help set off this covered outdoor living area.

Slate tiles, above, are a favorite material for patios and walks.

Using varying sizes of natural stone, right, adds a great deal of design interest to the area.

CHAPTER 9

REPAIRS & MAINTENANCE

Ceramic tile is durable and easy to maintain. However, aging tiles and grout joints eventually may crack, chip, or work loose, and need repair or replacement.

Grout is often the weak link in both floors and walls. It generally attracts mildew and discolors more easily than tile. Grout is also more likely than tile to crack from minor structural settling and other everyday stresses in the building frame. Most homeowners are familiar with these weak links. Some of them, such as the seams around a tub, can be chronic maintenance problems.

When a tile joint opens in a wet area like that, you can't afford to put off repairs. An open grout joint allows water to seep in and work under the tile. That can break the adhesive bond over a wood subfloor and begin to rot the supporting plywood. And as layers of the plywood weaken and separate, they're likely to cause more cracks.

In extreme cases where the structural support for tile gives way, you may have to scrap part of the existing floor or wall and start from scratch.

Routine Cleaning

For day-to-day cleaning, simply wipe down tile with warm water and a sponge. On floors, regular sweeping or vacuuming should prevent dirt and grit from scratching the tile surface and grinding into grout joints.

There are many proprietary tile cleaners that can remove light buildups of dirt, grease, soap scum, and water spots. For stubborn stains, try a strong solution of soap-free, all-purpose cleaner or a commercial tile cleaner. Don't use acid-based cleaners; they can attack grout. Always rinse thoroughly with clean water. Unglazed tiles should be resealed after cleaning. **1–5.**

If you *really* need to scour the surface, use a woven-plastic pot scrubber rather than steel wool, which sheds flecks of metal that leave rust stains in grout joints. Avoid using soap-based detergents because they generally dull the tile surface. Remember not to mix different types of cleaners, and never mix ammonia with bleach or products that contain it. That combination can produce lethal fumes.

Removing Common Stains

Strong solutions of all-purpose cleaners or commercial tile cleaners will remove most stains. (Find suggestions for removing some of the more unusual stains in the adjacent stain removal chart.) But in most households there are two common cleaning problems: mold on tile grout, and a buildup of soap scum that's sometimes combined with hard-water scale.

To clean grout joints, first rinse the area with water. Then use a toothbrush dipped in household bleach to remove stains. Stubborn stains may respond to a preliminary dose of straight bleach. If the grout is colored, test a spot to make sure the bleach will not cause discoloration. If it does, use a commercial tub-and-tile cleaner. Use household bleach with caution: wear rubber gloves and safety glasses. (See page 192, **1–3.**)

Another option is to try a combination of household bleach and an abrasive cleanser (one that does not contain ammonia). Make a paste, scrub it on, and rinse. If some spots remain, cover them with a wet mound of the paste for several hours before scrubbing again. To tackle a stain that is deep in the grout, try a soupy poultice of baking soda and liquid detergent mounded up and left on the spot overnight to draw out the stain. Don't try to grind away blemishes with abrasives that can cut into the tile glaze.

To remove mild soap deposits and hard-water spots, spray the surfaces with an all-purpose, nonabrasive cleaner, and let it soak in for a few minutes before rinsing. If some deposits remain, mist the area with vinegar, and let it sit for a few minutes before wiping. If all else fails try a proprietary soap-scum or mineral-deposit remover.

Hard-Water Problems

If you are concerned mainly with mineral deposits in water that form white scale, check into the problem yourself with a water-hardness test kit, or try this simple home test. Add ten drops of liquid detergent to half a glass of tap water, cover, and shake. If the detergent forms high, foamy suds, you have relatively soft water and probably don't need water-conditioning equipment. If the detergent forms low, curdled suds, you have relatively hard water and probably could benefit from a water-softening system.

Stain Removal Chart

Stain	Removal Agent
Grease & fats	Household cleaners
Tar, asphalt, oil, grease, oil paints, petroleum-based products	**Indoors:** Charcoal lighter fluid; then household cleaner, water rinse **Outdoors:** Concrete cleaner
Ink, mustard, blood, lipstick, merthiolate, coffee, tea, fruit juices, colored dyes	**Mild:** 3% hydrogen peroxide **Deep:** Household bleach
Nail polish	**Wet:** Charcoal lighter fluid **Dry:** Nail polish remover
Liquid medicines, shellac	Denatured alcohol
Rust	Rust remover; then household cleaner; rinse
Chewing gum	Chill with ice wrapped in cloth; scrape off surface

Caution: Some cleaning agents are toxic, caustic, or flammable. Use only as directed by the manufacturer and with adequate protective gear.

Basic Cleaning

Tools and Materials   Easy

- Vacuum cleaner or broom
- Cleanser
- Bucket
- Scrub brush and sponge
- Roller and tile sealer
- Rubber gloves

TILE TIP: *Unglazed tiles may take several hours to dry after a wet cleaning and look blotchy until they do.*

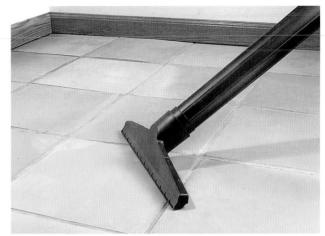

1 *Sweep or vacuum a tile floor before scrubbing with a cleanser to avoid grinding surface dust and grit into the tile glaze.*

2 *Although there are many specialized tile cleaners and stain removers, a mild solution of cleanser and water handles general cleanup.*

3 *Use a scrub brush with soft bristles on stubborn stains. If you use bleach on tough stains, wear rubber gloves and safety glasses.*

4 *Rinse the floor after cleaning to remove any cleanser residue. Regularly wring out the sponge and change the rinse water.*

5 *You can apply a sealer over a dry, clean floor of unglazed tiles. This helps to protect both the tile and the grout joints.*

Routine Maintenance

Sealing Grout & Unglazed Tile

You can apply a clear sealer to the grout joints only, or to the entire floor, if you have unglazed tiles. A sealer doesn't eliminate cleaning and periodic repairs, but it does add a measure of protection against stains. You may find that some sealers darken the tile a bit in the same way that a clear coating can slightly change the hue of brick or concrete in a patio.

The drawback is that you need to reapply the sealer about every two years (or as specified by the manufacturer) to maintain protection. And before you can roll out another coating, you'll need to clean the tile and grout thoroughly and allow the floor to dry completely.

Optional Waxing

Many tile waxes and buffing compounds are available for unglazed tile floors. Some are colored to enhance the appearance of unglazed terra-cotta tiles or pavers. After cleaning the floor with a soap-free floor cleaner and rinsing thoroughly with clear water, let the surface dry, and buff out the existing wax to restore the shine. When it's time to reapply wax, you'll need to strip off any old wax, wash the floor with a mild detergent, and rinse thoroughly with clear water. Two or three light coats of wax look better than one heavy coat.

The drawback is that a buffed wax finish can make tile floors slippery. You have to decide whether the improved appearance and protection is worth the increased risk of an accidental slip or fall.

Cleaning Old Grout

Tools and Materials   Easy

- Household bleach
- Scrub brush
- Grout sealer
- Applicator or artist's brush
- Rubber gloves and safety glasses

TILE TIP: *Remember that straight bleach may discolor the surface of unglazed tile. You should test a small section to see the result.*

1 Few specialized cleaners can match the effectiveness of straight household bleach on mold-stained grout. Test a small section on dark grout.

2 Let a puddle of bleach sit for a few minutes on the most stubborn stains. Brushing can help to dislodge deep stains in porous grout.

3 Once the grout is clean and dry, reduce further staining (and cleaning) by coating grout seams with a clear sealer.

Maintaining Tub Surrounds

If you spill water on a tile counter or floor, you'll probably wipe it up. But the tile and grout around tubs and showers get soaked and stay wet on a regular basis. This makes the area difficult to keep clean and a prime candidate for a complete overhaul. (See the complete how-to sequence on the following pages.)

Often the most troublesome location is the seam between the wall tiles and the edges of the tub. One reason for trouble: some do-it-yourselfers grout this seam along with the rest of the tile joints instead of filling it with caulk. A liberal bead of flexible silicone caulk helps to shed water. It also bridges the gap between the wall tiles, which are subject to one set of stresses, and the tub, which is subject to another.

A combination of wall and floor tile can provide an easy-cleaning, low-maintenance environment.

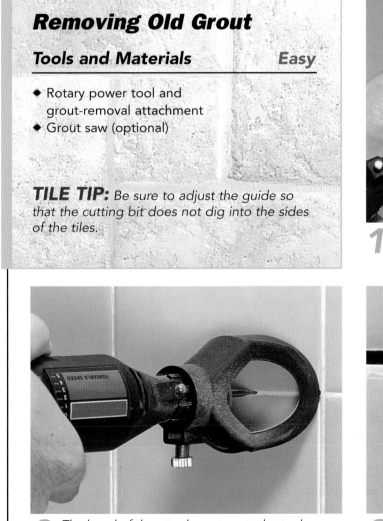

Removing Old Grout

Tools and Materials   *Easy*

◆ Rotary power tool and grout-removal attachment
◆ Grout saw (optional)

TILE TIP: *Be sure to adjust the guide so that the cutting bit does not dig into the sides of the tiles.*

1 *Grout-removal attachments are typically sold as accessories for rotary-type power tools. The guide hood clamps over the chuck.*

2 *The hood of the attachment seats the tool on the tile, while guide nibs keep the cutter aligned with the grout seam.*

3 *With a grout-removal attachment, you can clean out the seams between tiles without damaging or dislodging the surrounding tiles.*

Repairing a Tiled Tub Surround

Tools and Materials   Easy

- Tile cleaner and applicator
- Hook scraper and razor cutter
- Grout mix, rubber float, squeegee, rag, and sponge
- Sealer, caulk, and caulking gun

TILE TIP: *Once the grout is cleaned (or replaced), taking the time to seal it will greatly reduce the need for more cleaning.*

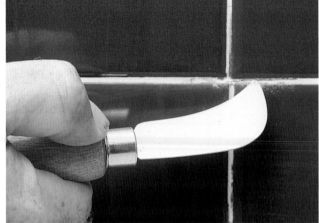

1 To scrape out damaged or deeply stained grout you can use a carpet knife, a small grout saw, or a power grout-removal tool. (See page 193.)

4 When the damaged grout is cleared and the joints are brushed clean, mix fresh grout to a workable, slightly soupy consistency.

5 Spread grout with strokes on the diagonal to the seams. Use a rubber-surfaced float for spreading and a squeegee for removing the excess.

8 To smooth out a bead of caulk, the not-very-high-tech tool that often works best is the end of your finger dipped in soapy water.

9 To prevent water from seeping behind the plumbing fixtures and under the tiles, also apply a thin bead of caulk around the fixture edges.

2 On many older installations you need to slice off one or more layers of old caulk and clean out the seam between the tile and the tub.

3 If you need to scrub stubborn soap scum or water deposits, use a sponge or plastic pad, not steel wool, which can cause rust stains.

6 When the grout sets up you can make the first of many passes with a clean, damp rag to remove extra residue and the final grout haze.

7 To create a waterproof seal between the bottom row of tiles and the tub, apply a continuous bead of a flexible, silicone-based caulk.

10 This grout calls for wet curing. You keep it damp by misting with water several times a day. Plastic sheets help contain the moisture.

11 To protect the new grout and reduce the need for future maintenance and repairs, seal the seams with clear silicone sealer.

Fixing Broken Tiles

You can break a damaged tile into small pieces that are easy to remove. But if surrounding tiles are solidly interlocked with grout, the reverberating forces of a hammer and cold chisel are likely to cause even more damage. A better approach in many cases is to remove the grout first.

Dislodging Tiles

One way to contain the project is to use hand tools with a minimum amount of force, digging and prying instead of hammering. For example, when a piece of tile is loose, you can carve out some grout and work a screwdriver under the section that still adheres to the subfloor.

If the tile is cracked but solidly set, drill a row of holes across the tile to create a fault line that will break with a few light taps. This exposes edges that you can more easily pry and lift.

If the tile is difficult to drill (even new masonry bits tend to skid on glazed surfaces) you can drill a series of small holes in the solid grout bordering the tile. **1.** The trick is to keep the bit centered and avoid damaging adjacent tiles as you drill. The holes make it easier to dig out the grout and expose the edges of the tile. If the surrounding grout is already loose, score the seams around the tile with a grout saw or utility knife, making repeated passes as needed to isolate the tile. **2.** Then use a narrow screwdriver to pry out the grout so you can work on the tile. With the grout gone, a cracked tile is easily pried up with a cold chisel or screwdriver tip. **3.**

Another approach is to use either a power grout-removing attachment on a rotary tool or a small grout saw to clear away the grout. Hand-held rotary tools (best known by the brand name Dremel) typically come in kits (for about $40) with a variety of bits and shapers. You can use one of the grinding bits to clear away grout, and a grout-removal attachment (about $20) to keep the bit centered in the seam. You can adjust the cutter to skim off a top layer of grout and prepare for regrouting, or use it at the full depth to carve away a grout seam and make it easy to remove adjacent tiles.

Setting Replacement Tile

Over floors, use a wood chisel to scrape and cut away any raised ribs of old adhesive. **4.** You don't have to remove all traces, but you do need to make room for a new layer of adhesive. Otherwise, the replacement tile will not embed enough to adhere properly, and may not set flush with the floor surface.

Over drywall, it's difficult to remove a tile without bringing along scraps of paper and some of the underlying gypsum. (Be sure to cut away any loose material with a utility knife before making a repair.)

On deep scars you can make a standard drywall patch with spackle, or simply set the new tile in a thick bed of adhesive. But if you apply a thick layer to fill drywall voids, you could push the tile below the wall surface, making it impossible to grout. So if you do take this shortcut, nestle the new tile in place and use masking tape to hold it flush with the surrounding wall surface.

Over any surface, work the new tile side to side to get a good bond, and leave it centered in the space to maintain even grout seams. **5.** Once the adhesive sets (usually overnight), you can add grout to finish the repair.

Replacing Broken Tiles

Tools and Materials   *Moderate*

- Drill and masonry bit
- Grout saw
- Cold chisel
- Wood chisel or scraper
- Tile adhesive and notched trowel

TILE TIP: *To avoid damage to surrounding tiles during a repair, isolate a damaged tile by cutting through and digging out the grout.*

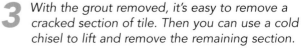

3 *With the grout removed, it's easy to remove a cracked section of tile. Then you can use a cold chisel to lift and remove the remaining section.*

Tile Tip Digging Out Grout

You can dig out grout with a cold chisel, or cut it away with a power grout-removal tool. (See how it works on page 193.) But there are two other methods to consider. You can simply drill out the grout by making a series of holes with a masonry bit, or cut it out with a small handheld grout saw that has an abrasive edge.

Hand grout saws have both abrasive and toothed cutting blades.

Masonry bits have an extended carbide tip to cut through grout.

1 Drill holes with a masonry bit near the corners of the damaged tile. This helps to isolate the tile and prevents damage to the surrounding area.

2 You can slice along the edge of the tile with a utility knife if necessary, and then dig out the grout with a grout saw.

4 To prepare the substrate, you need to scrape away any raised ribs of old adhesive that could prevent the new tile from seating.

5 Once the substrate is leveled, spread new tile adhesive with the end of a notched trowel, and set the replacement tile in position.

Fixing Trapped Tiles

Tiles that crack in the middle of a floor are easy enough to replace. But the job becomes more difficult when part of the tile is trapped beneath a cabinet, sink, toilet, or other fixture that you can't or don't want to remove. Trapped-tile repairs can be tricky. But it's possible to make a repair that will look as though you replaced the entire tile without removing the fixture.

Start by clearing out the grout around the broken tile. **1–2.** Then score and carefully cut along the seam between the tile and the trapping fixture, and remove the exposed portion of the damaged tile. **3–4.** The next step is to mark and cut a replacement tile that will nestle against the fixture. You can mark the new tile by transferring the fixture outline with a contour gauge or a compass. **5.** Then cut the replacement on a wet saw, or use a snap cutter and tile nippers, as the shape requires. **6.**

Scrape the old adhesive off the substrate, apply a new ribbed layer of adhesive, and set the replacement. **7.** Use masking tape to secure it until the adhesive sets. Grout the tile, and caulk the exposed seam between the tile and fixture. **8.**

Where tiles butt against fixtures, you should apply a bead of flexible caulk to seal the seams.

Replacing Trapped Tiles

Tools and Materials   Moderate

- Drill and masonry bit
- Cold chisel or screwdriver
- Glass cutter or cutting wheel tool
- Compass or contour gauge
- Wet saw or snap cutter and tile nippers
- Adhesive, caulk, and caulking gun

TILE TIP: To mark a glazed tile, try a grease pencil. Its mark will stay, whereas a lead pencil won't transfer, and a pen can easily smudge.

3 Start the cut between the fixture and the trapped tile by scoring the surface. A glass cutter may help, but a cutting wheel works better.

6 To create the cleanest possible cuts for the butt joints, use a wet saw wherever possible. Next best is a snap cutter and tile nippers.

1 Isolate the damaged tile by drilling holes in the surrounding grout joints. You may also need to score between the tiles with a utility knife.

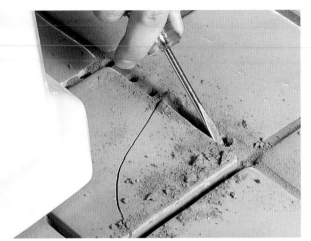

2 Dig out the grout around the tile, starting in the corner and working your way along the seam with a narrow screwdriver or cold chisel.

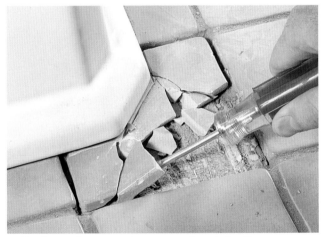

4 Once the grout is removed and the fixture seam is scored (or cut through completely), you can break out the remaining sections of exposed tile.

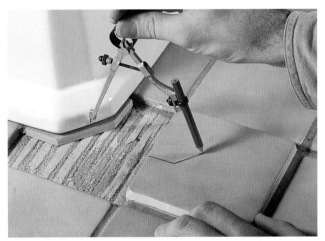

5 Align a new tile on the grid next to the damaged area, and transfer the fixture outline with a compass. You might use a contour gauge instead.

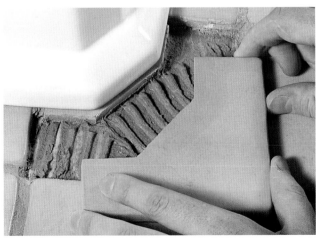

7 Scrape old adhesive off the substrate to make way for the replacement. Then apply a ribbed bed of adhesive and set the new tile.

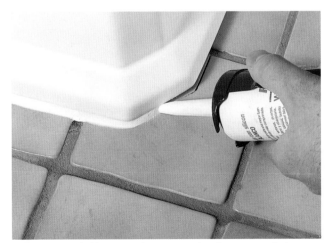

8 To seal the joints between the fixture and the new cut tile, add a thin bead of flexible, silicone-based caulk along the seams.

APPENDIX
■ ■ ■

TILE
INSTALLATION SPECS

For many of us, installing tile isn't all that complicated. We just figure out where we want to put it, what tile we want to use, and when we're going to find the time and money to wrap everything up. As long as we don't venture far from the typical tile job, life is good.

But what if we want to cover a concrete patio with bluestone, or embed some radiant heat under a new bathroom floor, or install an outdoor shower and want to match the tile on the swimming pool apron? For jobs like these, we need the installation specifications that are produced for architects, engineers, and tradespeople.

We found installation details on just about every tile job under the sun at The Tile Council Of North America (www.tileusa.com). The drawings in this chapter are all based on TCA research and focus on some of the less common residential tile jobs. If you need something special, look here. If you can't find it, go to TCA's Web site.

DESIGN DETAILS FOR TILE FLOORS OVER CONCRETE SLABS

A properly installed concrete slab, whether outside or in, is a durable high-quality structure that can yield many years of service with little or no problems. Durable, yes; but attractive, well...

It's fair to say that not everyone thinks concrete is beautiful. And because of this, many different strategies for covering up all the slabs in our life have been developed. Certainly two of the most popular, in both the commercial and residential worlds, are carpet and tile.

Carpet is usually the choice where a softer, more forgiving surface is desired. But carpet requires a lot of routine maintenance, and it wears out. A good tile installation, on the other hand, can last indefinitely and only needs a little soap and water when it gets dirty.

There are nearly as many ways to install tile over a concrete slab as there are baseball teams in the major leagues. This book has previously explained the most common techniques. But to provide some sense of the variety of installation methods, we've included five additional approaches shown here.

Drawing **#1** shows ceramic tile over an exterior slab. This traditional approach includes a 1¼-in.-thick bed of mortar on top of the slab and an optional waterproof membrane over the mortar. This is a job better suited to a contractor than a homeowner. Proper installation of a thick mortar bed can be difficult.

Drawing **#2** shows the same exterior slab with the optional waterproof membrane. But in this case, the tile is bonded to the concrete with an easy-to-install thinset (either dry-set or latex) mortar.

Drawings **#3** and **#4** show the companion installations for interior concrete slabs. The first features the thick mortar bed, while the second uses thinset or latex mortar to set the tile. Both approaches omit the optional waterproof membrane shown in **#1** and **#2**.

Drawing **#5** is identical to **#4**, but it features an organic adhesive instead of a thinset mortar. The organic adhesive is easier to use, and it dries by evaporation (which is quicker) instead of curing, as is the case with mortar.

1. Exterior Tile Floor on Mortar Bed over Concrete Slab

Thinset

Waterproof Membrane

Gravel

Mortar Bed

Concrete Slab

2. Exterior Tile Floor on Concrete Slab

Thinset

Waterproof Membrane

Gravel

Concrete Slab

3. Interior Tile Floor on Mortar Bed over Concrete Slab

Concrete

Mortar Bed

Thinset

4. Interior Tile Floor on Concrete Slab

Concrete

Thinset

5. Interior Tile Floor in Adhesive on Concrete Slab

Concrete

Organic Adhesive

DESIGN DETAILS FOR TILE FLOORS OVER WOOD SUBFLOORS

In most houses, a wood subfloor forms the base material for nearly all ceramic floor tile installations. These include the big three: kitchen, bathroom, and powder room floors. But tile is also the default floor finish for foyers, mudrooms, and pantries. The biggest difference between a concrete and a wood subfloor is stability. The concrete, at least in interior installations, is very stable. Wood (usually plywood) is less stable. The tile installation specs take this into account, as you can see in the drawings here.

Drawing **#1** shows the tile in a substantial mortar bed reinforced with metal lath. The reinforcement and the weight of this mortar bed make it very stable. In Drawing **#2** you see a much easier installation. To install the tile, all that's needed is organic adhesive. But to stabilize the floor you must have a double layer of ⅝-in.-thick exterior-grade plywood.

You can achieve the stability of the double layers of plywood by substituting a cementitious backer board for the top underlayment layer of plywood as shown in Drawing **#3.** When properly installed, the backer board provides better water resistance and is therefore a good choice for wet areas.

For damp areas, some tile contractors substitute the cementitious backer board in **#3** with a water-resistant gypsum backer board shown in Drawing **#4.** This material is for indoor use only and for areas that are occasionally damp, not frequently wet.

One of the best alternatives to a mortar bed base is shown in Drawing **#5.** Instead of using extra plywood or backer boards for a stable base, this installation features a poured gypsum underlayment. This material is installed as a thick liquid and is nearly self-leveling. Once it's dry you have a very smooth, uniform base that's ideal for laying tile.

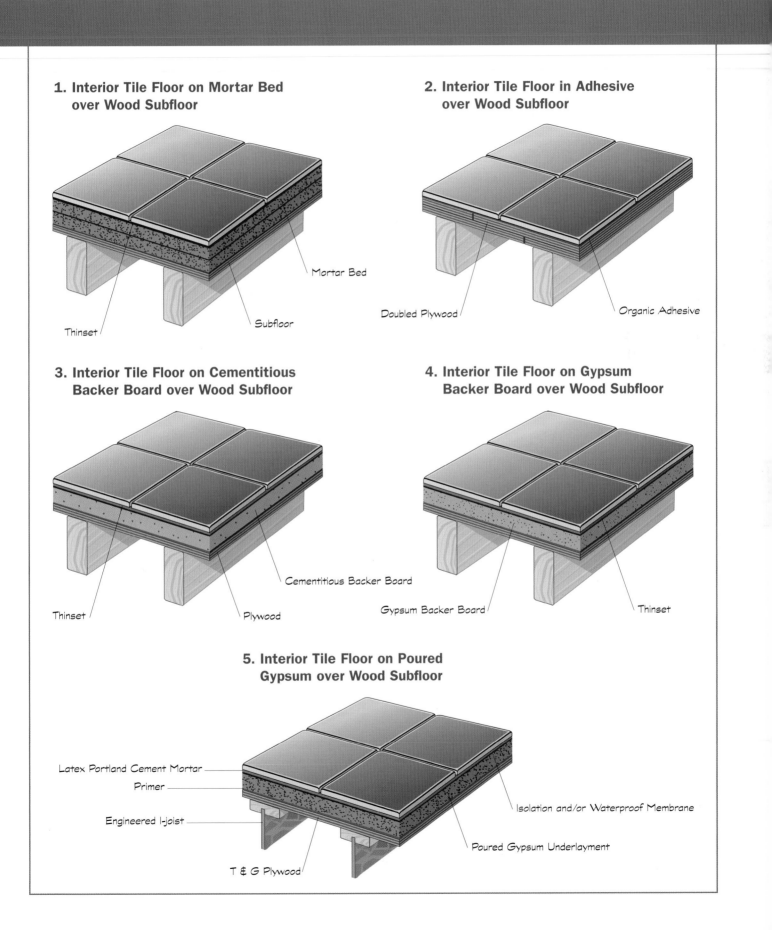

1. Interior Tile Floor on Mortar Bed over Wood Subfloor

Mortar Bed

Subfloor

Thinset

2. Interior Tile Floor in Adhesive over Wood Subfloor

Doubled Plywood

Organic Adhesive

3. Interior Tile Floor on Cementitious Backer Board over Wood Subfloor

Cementitious Backer Board

Thinset

Plywood

4. Interior Tile Floor on Gypsum Backer Board over Wood Subfloor

Gypsum Backer Board

Thinset

5. Interior Tile Floor on Poured Gypsum over Wood Subfloor

Latex Portland Cement Mortar

Primer

Engineered I-joist

Isolation and/or Waterproof Membrane

Poured Gypsum Underlayment

T & G Plywood

DESIGN DETAILS FOR TILE FLOORS OVER RADIANT HEAT

Over the last 15 years, in-floor radiant heat has grown from a niche heating system to one that's practically ubiquitous. There are several good reasons why it's nice to have radiant heat around. It warms rooms evenly; it doesn't need a loud blower to push air through a tangled system of ducts; and it keeps your feet toasty whether you're in the bathroom, the living room, or the basement.

Radiant heat has made tile floors more popular and forced the development of new installation specs to keep things running right. Five of these approaches are shown here. The first deals with a hydronic (hot water) radiant system. The other four feature electric-resistance radiant heat.

Hydronic in-floor heat is the traditional approach that's been around for decades. As you can see in Drawing **#1,** the tile installation is pretty simple. Pouring a concrete slab around the water heating pipes is another matter. In Drawing **#2** the installation of the electric radiant heat is a little easier: it's embedded in mortar over a standard slab. Once the mortar is cured, the tile job is very straightforward.

When the radiant heat goes over a wood subfloor instead of a concrete slab, installation options start expanding. In Drawing **#3** you see electric radiant components surrounded by a poured gypsum underlayment. The gypsum provides a beautiful, flat surface for installing the tile.

In Drawing **#4** the heating components are embedded in latex mortar over a double layer of plywood subfloor. The EGP designation on the mortar stands for "exterior glue plywood," which means that the mortar has an additive that makes it bond very well to the plywood subfloor.

Drawing **#5** shows nearly the same approach as **#4.** But in this case, a cementitious backer board takes the place of the underlayment layer of subfloor plywood. The tile is installed the same way in both cases.

1. Tile Floor over Slab with Hydronic Radiant Heat

2. Tile Floor over Slab with Electric Radiant Heat in Mortar Bed

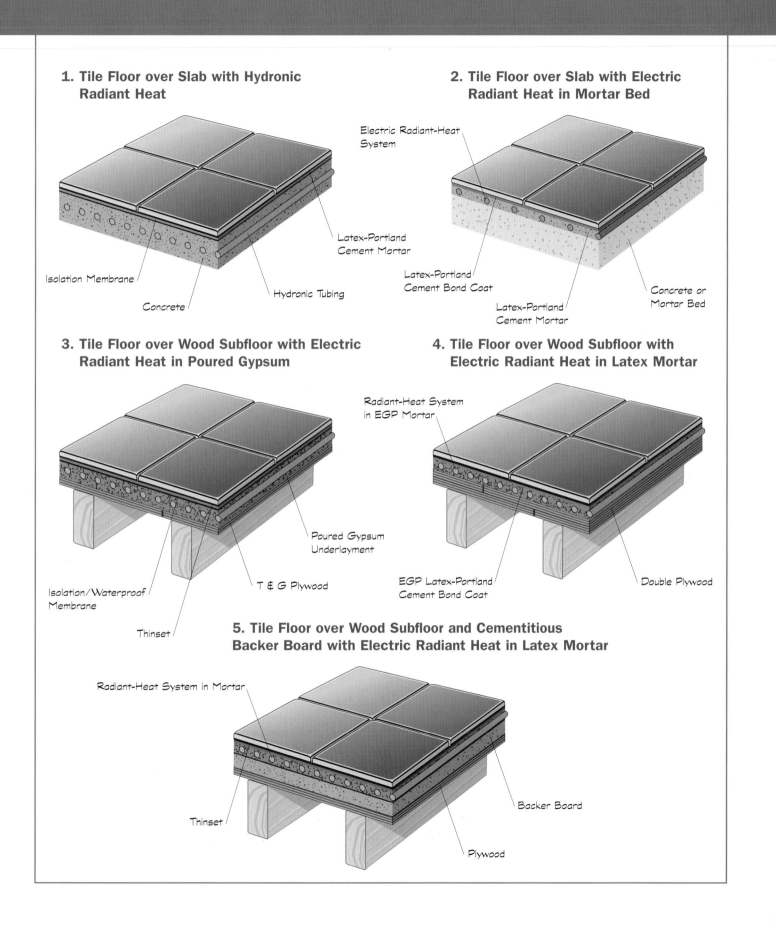

Isolation Membrane

Concrete

Hydronic Tubing

Latex-Portland Cement Mortar

Electric Radiant-Heat System

Latex-Portland Cement Bond Coat

Latex-Portland Cement Mortar

Concrete or Mortar Bed

3. Tile Floor over Wood Subfloor with Electric Radiant Heat in Poured Gypsum

4. Tile Floor over Wood Subfloor with Electric Radiant Heat in Latex Mortar

Isolation/Waterproof Membrane

Thinset

T & G Plywood

Poured Gypsum Underlayment

Radiant-Heat System in EGP Mortar

EGP Latex-Portland Cement Bond Coat

Double Plywood

5. Tile Floor over Wood Subfloor and Cementitious Backer Board with Electric Radiant Heat in Latex Mortar

Radiant-Heat System in Mortar

Thinset

Backer Board

Plywood

DESIGN DETAILS FOR TILE WALLS

Generally speaking, tile walls are not exposed to the same amount of abuse that tile floors suffer. This happy fact is sponsored by our good friends at gravity. None of us walks on a wall, at least not all day long. And water never pools on a wall and then tries to attack the mortar or adhesive underneath that holds everything together. Because of this, you might think that tiling a wall would be easier than working on a floor. Unfortunately, most of the time it's not, because the same gravity that keeps weight and water off a wall wants to pull the wall into a pile of debris on the floor.

A quick look at Drawing **#1** will show you that things haven't gotten much easier. A typical exterior masonry wall must first be covered with a mortar bed that's reinforced with metal lath. Only when this bed is cured can the tile be attached with thinset mortar. If an exterior masonry wall is sound and very flat you can use the easier method shown in Drawing **#2.** This just calls for thinset mortar between the tile and the wall.

Another approach is shown in Drawing **#3.** Here, an interior masonry wall that has a rough, uneven surface must be tiled. The best choice is to apply a smooth mortar bed over the wall surface. When this is cured, the tile can be installed with thinset mortar or adhesive.

Drawings **#4** and **#5** show two good ways to tile over walls built with wood or metal studs. In **#4** gypsum board is specified as the base and in **#5** a cementitious backer board is installed. The gypsum method is only appropriate for dry conditions. But if a waterproof membrane is added to the backer-board installation, it can be used in wet or dry areas.

1. Exterior Tile Wall on Mortar Bed over Masonry Wall

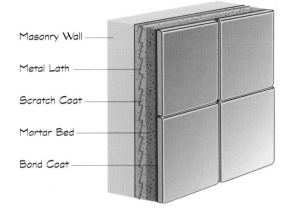

Masonry Wall

Metal Lath

Scratch Coat

Mortar Bed

Bond Coat

2. Exterior Tile Wall on Latex Mortar Bed over Masonry Wall

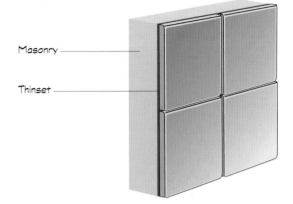

Masonry

Thinset

3. Interior Tile Wall on Mortar Bed over Masonry Wall

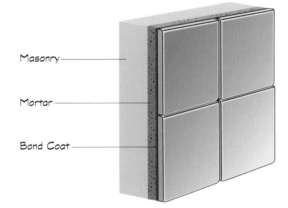

Masonry

Mortar

Bond Coat

4. Interior Tile Wall on Gypsum Board over Wood or Metal Studs

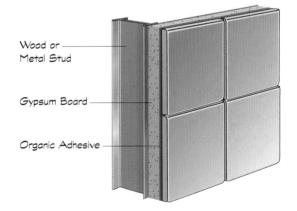

Wood or Metal Stud

Gypsum Board

Organic Adhesive

5. Interior Tile Wall on Water-Resistant Backer Board over Wood or Metal Studs

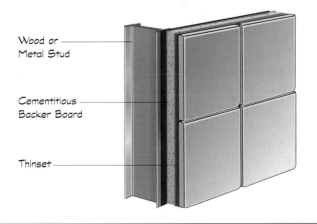

Wood or Metal Stud

Cementitious Backer Board

Thinset

DESIGN DETAILS FOR TILE CEILINGS, TUB AND SHOWER WALLS, COUNTERTOPS, AND TILE-OVER-TILE RENOVATIONS

A ceiling may not be the first place that most of us install tile, but commercial installations have used tile ceilings forever. Just think about the gym shower rooms when you were a kid. One of the most common approaches is shown in Drawing **#1.** The wood framing is simply covered with gypsum board, and the tile is attached with adhesive or thinset mortar.

Tiling the walls above bathtubs and shower stalls is another common tile job. Drawings **#2** and **#3** show the typical approaches: **#2** calls for a base of water-resistant gypsum board, while **#3** features a cementitious backer-board base. In both cases, the bottom course of tile does not rest on the lip of the tub or shower unit. Space is left for flexible sealant (caulk) between the materials.

Kitchen and bath countertops are two more places where tile is very popular. Several sections in this book feature different countertop treatments. The methods shown in Drawing **#4** are practically the default choices for most jobs. The countertop is made of plywood that's covered with a membrane, followed by backer board, thinset mortar, and tile.

A great way to update old, or slightly damaged, tile without making a lot of mess is to cover the old tile directly with new tile. This process is usually called a tile-over-tile renovation. The four drawings shown here, **#5A, #5B, #5C,** and **#5D,** indicate four different approaches. In each case, the new tile is bonded to the old with thinset mortar or adhesive.

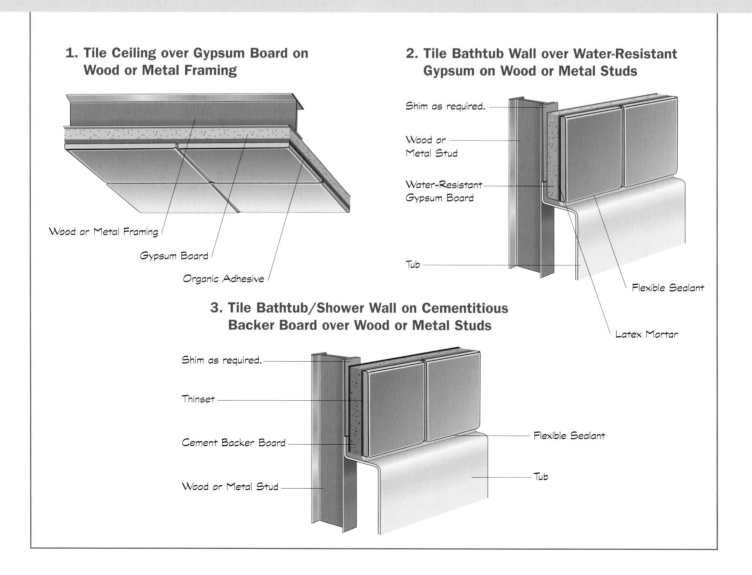

1. Tile Ceiling over Gypsum Board on Wood or Metal Framing

Wood or Metal Framing
Gypsum Board
Organic Adhesive

2. Tile Bathtub Wall over Water-Resistant Gypsum on Wood or Metal Studs

Shim as required.
Wood or Metal Stud
Water-Resistant Gypsum Board
Tub
Flexible Sealant
Latex Mortar

3. Tile Bathtub/Shower Wall on Cementitious Backer Board over Wood or Metal Studs

Shim as required.
Thinset
Cement Backer Board
Wood or Metal Stud
Flexible Sealant
Tub

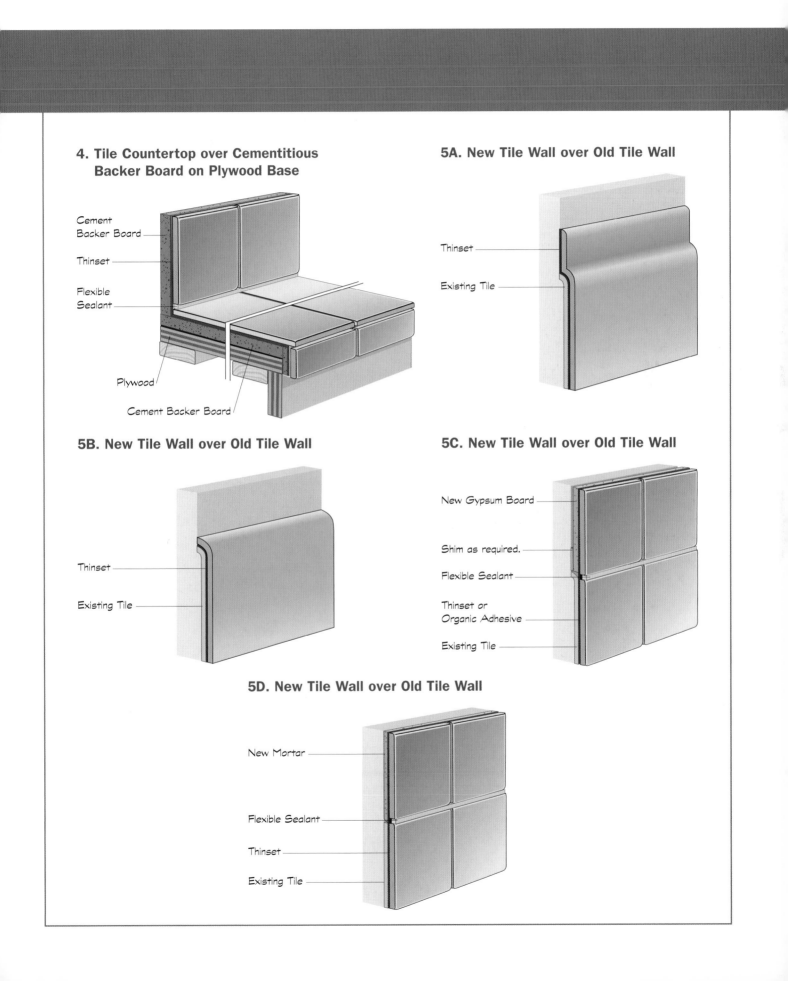

4. Tile Countertop over Cementitious Backer Board on Plywood Base

Cement Backer Board

Thinset

Flexible Sealant

Plywood

Cement Backer Board

5A. New Tile Wall over Old Tile Wall

Thinset

Existing Tile

5B. New Tile Wall over Old Tile Wall

Thinset

Existing Tile

5C. New Tile Wall over Old Tile Wall

New Gypsum Board

Shim as required.

Flexible Sealant

Thinset or Organic Adhesive

Existing Tile

5D. New Tile Wall over Old Tile Wall

New Mortar

Flexible Sealant

Thinset

Existing Tile

RESOURCE GUIDE

The following list of manufacturers and associations is meant to be a general guide to additional industry and product-related sources. It is not intended as a listing of products and manufacturers represented by the photographs in this book.

American Marazzi
359 Clay Rd.
Sunnyvale, TX 75182
972-226-0110
www.marazzitile.com
American Marazzi manufactures an extensive line of floor and wall tile.

American Olean
www.aotile.com
American Olean manufactures ceramic tile for floors, walls, and countertops. The company's Web site features a number of design tools.

American Slate Company
611 Industrial Ave.
Boynton Beach, FL 33426
561-742-0200
www.americanslate.com
American Slate Company offers slate and quartzite tiles for floors, roofs, walls, fireplaces, and countertops.

Bosch Tools
877-267-2499
www.boschtools.com
Bosch manufactures power tools, including corded and cordless drills, sanders, saws, and other specialty tools.

Ceramic Tile Institute of America, Inc.
12061 W. Jefferson Blvd.
Culver City, CA 90230
310-574-7800
www.ctioa.org
The Ceramic Tile Institute of America supports the expanded use of ceramic tile and is a good source of information about tiling.

Craftsman Tools
Sears
3333 Beverly Rd.
Hoffman Estates, IL 60179
www.craftsman.com
Craftsman sells more tools than any other retailer. Through an extensive chain of outlets, Craftsman offers a wide variety of basic tools and tile specialty tools.

Crossville, Inc.

P.O. Box 1168
Crossville, TN 38557
931-484-2110
www.crossvilleinc.com
Crossville, Inc., manufactures an expansive selection of residential tile in a variety of styles, colors, and sizes.

Custom Building Products

13001 Seal Beach Blvd.
Seal Beach, CA 90740
800-272-8786
www.custombuildingproducts.com
Custom Building Products' extensive line of construction materials and tools includes thinset mortar mix, organic mastic, grout, and grout sealers.

Daltile

7834 C.F. Hawn Frwy.
Dallas, TX 75217
214-398-1411
www.daltile.com
Daltile offers an inventory of ceramic tile for kitchens, baths, and entryways, as well as for outdoor applications such as pools and spas.

Deutsche Steinzeug America, Inc.

367 Curie Dr.
Alpaharetta, GA 30005
770-442-5500
www.dsa-ceramics.com
Deutsche Steinzeug America, Inc., manufactures tiles coated with Hydrotect, a protective finish that, according to the company, guarantees brilliant cleanliness with a minimum of cleaning effort.

Fraser Clay Works, Inc.

64 Myrtlewood Dr.
Mountain Home, AR 72653
870-492-5031
www.fraserclayworks.com
Fraser specializes in high-relief hand-crafted wall tiles.

Hitachi Power Tools

www.hitachipowertools.com
Hitachi manufactures innovative power tools, including cordless drills, pneumatics, and special tools for concrete and masonry.

Hyde Manufacturing Company

54 Eastford Rd.
Southbridge, MA 01550
800-USA-HYDE
www.hydetools.com
Hyde makes a wide variety of hand tools for masonry and drywall, and tools for setting and finishing tile, such as spackle blades and floats for applying grout.

Makita Industrial Power Tools

800-462-5482
www.makita.com
Makita manufactures power tools, including a full line of cordless drills.

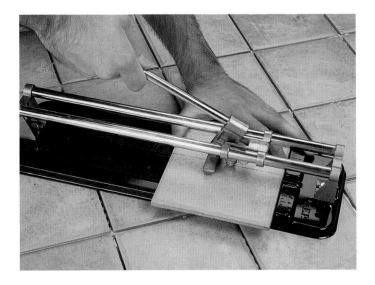

Motawi TileWorks

170 Enterprise Dr.
Ann Arbor, MI 48103
734-213-0017
www.motawi.com
Motawi manufactures decorative tile in assorted sizes and shapes.

National Association of the Remodeling Industry (NARI)

4900 Seminary Road, Ste. 320
Arlington, VA 22311
703-575-1100
www.remodeltoday.com
This organization represents thousands of home improvement professionals and offers consumers links to NARI-certified local contractors.

National Concrete Masonry Association

2302 Horse Pen Rd.
Herndon, VA 20171
703-713-1900
www.ncma.org
This trade group representing the concrete masonry industry offers a variety of technical service, design aids, and publications.

National Kitchen & Bath Association

687 Willow Grove St.
Hackettstown, NJ 07840
908-852-0033
www.nkba.org
This national organization supplies design and planning information for kitchen and bath projects and referrals to professionals.

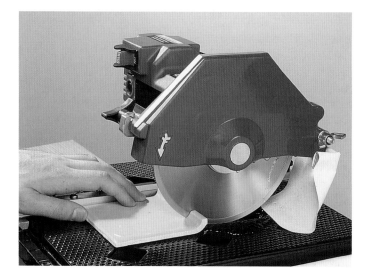

Q.E.P. Co., Inc.

1081 Holland Dr.
Boca Raton, FL 33487
561-994-5550
www.qep.com
Q.E.P. Co., Inc., manufactures a broad line of flooring-related tools for both DIY and professional installers. These include trowels, floats, wet saws, and snap cutters.

National Fire Protection Association

1 Batterymarch Park
P.O. Box 9101
Quincy, MA 02269
617-770-3000
www.nfpa.org
This national group provides a wide variety of information on fire-safe construction.

The Noble Company

614 Monroe St.
P.O. Box 350
Grand Haven, MI 49417
231-799-8000
www.noblecompany.com
A manufacturer of Chloraloy brand CPE flexible membrane
material, used to waterproof tile installations in showers and tubs.

Porter-Cable Tools

4825 Hwy. 45 N.
P.O. Box 2468
Jackson, TN 38302
800-487-8665
www.porter-cable.com
A tool company with a variety of corded and cordless drills,
saws, sanders, and specialty tools.

Ryobi Tools

800-525-2579
www.ryobitools.com
Ryobi features an extensive line of power tools for every home
improvement project.

TEC Specialty Products, Inc.

315 S. Hicks Rd.
Palatine, IL 60067
800-832-9002
www.tecspecialty.com
TEC Specialty Products supplies a wide range of flooring
adhesives and surface-preparation products, including mortar,
grout, and joint sealants.

Tile Council of America, Inc.

100 Clemson Research Blvd.
Anderson, SC 29625
864-646-8453
www.tileusa.com
This trade group represents hundreds of tile companies and
offers a variety of information on tile, including the
Handbook for Ceramic Tile Installaton.

U.S. Gypsum Corp.

1254 South Franklin St.
Chicago, IL 60680
800-874-4968
www.usg.com
A major supplier of gypsum-based products, including
drywall, joint compound, backer board, and other tile-
installation and substrate supplies.

Zircon Corporation

1580 Dell Ave.
Campbell, CA 95008
800-245-9265
www.zircon.com
Zircon manufactures electronic hand tools, including measuring tools, laser levels, and stud sensors.

GLOSSARY

Apron tile   Tile set along the face of a structure—for example, along the front of a countertop edge or the vertical border of a sloping kitchen range hood.

Backer board   Cement-based sheet material used as a substrate for tile on walls, floors, and counters. The material of choice in any wet area such as a kitchen or bathroom because it is unaffected by water. Also called cementitious backer units, or CBUs.

Backer board cutting tool   A carbide-tipped hand tool used to score cement-based backer board so that it can be snapped to the proper size.

Backsplash   The vertical surface at the back of a countertop.

Bedding block   A block of wood (usually a 2×4) wrapped in carpeting or other padding used to level a high tile with the tiles around it.

Bridging   Supports attached between joists to increase rigidity of a floor. You can purchase steel bridging or make your own from common dimensional lumber.

Bullnose tile   A trim tile with at least one rounded-over edge used to finish outside corners.

Buttering   Applying adhesive with a trowel to the back of a tile to supplement the adhesive spread on the setting bed or substrate.

Caulk   One of many flexible compounds used to fill gaps between construction materials. Some key tile joints are filled with caulk instead of grout.

Cement-bodied tile   Tiles made of mortar instead of clay, generally providing the appearance of stone or pavers without a surface glaze.

Chalk-line box   A long string wound in a box filled with colored chalk used to mark straight layout lines by snapping against floors or walls.

Contour gauge   A tool used for duplicating complex shapes, such as moldings, onto tile, which then can be cut to fit.

Control joint   A shallow groove cut into the surface of a concrete slab before it hardens to confine small stress cracks. Minor cracks form down in the grooves instead of in the slab surface.

Course   One horizontal row of tiles or other materials.

Cove tile   A shaped trim tile with a slightly curved base that creates a rounded joint between adjacent walls, a wall and a floor, or other surfaces that meet at right angles. Often used as a sanitary detail along the bottom of bathroom walls.

CPE   Chlorinated polyethylene membrane, a flexible, rubbery sheet commonly used instead of lead or other materials to waterproof the floor of a tile shower or tub.

Curing   The period of time that concrete, tile adhesive, or grout must be left in order for it to reach its working strength. Curing time is usually longer than drying time.

Expansion joint   A space left between two surfaces that allows for natural expansion and contraction, typically filled with a flexible backer rod covered with caulk.

Field tile   A full-size tile in the main area of the installation.

Float   A long-handled tool used to smooth a concrete surface. More generally with tile, a term describing the process of shaping and smoothing a bed of mortar with a trowel.

Floated bed   A bed of mortar, often with a slope or other irregular shape, that serves as the setting surface for tile.

Forms   Structures usually made of 2×6s or other framing lumber to contain concrete as it cures.

Glaze   A hard surface generally fired onto the exposed side of a ceramic tile, which imparts a glossy shine.

Greenboard   A water-resistant variety of drywall used in kitchens and bathrooms.

Grout   A slurry troweled into joints between tiles that fills the seams and solidifies the tile field. Available in many formulas and colors.

Grout float A rubber-surfaced trowel used to apply grout to tiled surfaces.

Grout sealer Typically a clear coating, such as silicone, used to protect porous grout and facilitate cleaning.

Layout stick A straight, long, narrow board marked in increments of tile widths and grout joints.

Lugs Small projections, also called nubs, formed into tile edges to maintain even spacing.

Mastic Common term for organic-based adhesives.

Mortar The mixture of sand, cement, and water used to float beds for tile.

Metal lath Light-gauge metal reinforcing sheets often used to strengthen mortar beds (thickset) under tile.

Mosaic Small tiles that are used to create a design or pattern, generally sold in preassembled sheets.

Mud Tile-setter's term for mortar applied in a setting bed.

Nonvitreous tile A porous tile that absorbs moisture and is not resistant to freeze-thaw cycles.

Notched trowel A metal trowel with notches along one or more sides used to rake out ribs of adhesive to a specified height.

Open time The length of time adhesive can stay on a surface before it dries out, skins over, and no longer forms an effective bond.

Organic mastic A premixed oil- or water-based tile adhesive generally with less bond strength and water resistance than other thinsets.

Pot life The maximum time that a mixed adhesive will stay flexible enough to spread and create a good bond.

Running bond A basic tile pattern that alters the standard grid alignment, with tiles on one course staggered one-half the tile width from the tiles in the course below.

Score To scratch or etch a cut line in a tile or other material so that it will break in a clean line.

Sheet-mounted tile Any small-size tile mounted with spaced grout seams to a sheet or mesh backer for easier application.

Shower-floor membrane A flexible waterproof material under tile that protects against leak damage by directing any water that seeps through seams into the weep holes of the shower drain.

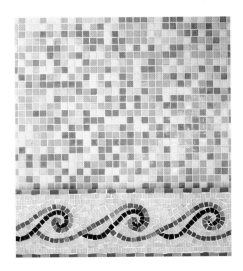

Snap cutter A hand-powered tile cutter with a scoring head that travels on metal guides and a raised rib over which the tile is snapped.

Squeegee A flexible, rubber-edge tool used to clean excess grout off a tiled surface.

Subfloor Plywood panels (or tongue-and-groove boards in older homes) installed over joists to support finished flooring material.

Substrate The supporting layer under tile, generally panels of plywood or backer board.

Thickset The term used for tile installations that use a thick bed of mortar between tile and substrate. Generally used on older installations, while thin beds of adhesive are generally used today.

Thinset The term for modern tile installations that use a thin ribbed coat of adhesive between the tile and substrate.

Thinset mortar The term generally used to describe any of the cement-based tile adhesives.

Tile nippers Similar to a pair of pliers, with strong biting blades used to break away small bits of tile to create cuts that are not in a straight line.

Tile spacers Cross-shaped pieces of plastic, available in many sizes, placed at the corners of newly laid tiles to maintain even spacing throughout a layout.

Underlayment Smooth panels of plywood or backer board used as a base for setting tile.

V-cap tile A basically L-shaped tile with a slightly raised corner commonly used along the edges of kitchen and bath countertops.

Vitreous tile A dense, strong, non-porous tile that is resistant to freeze-thaw cycles.

Wet saw A power tool with a circular, diamond-edged blade that trims individual tiles. The blade is lubricated by a stream of water that is collected in a pan beneath the tile and recirculated.

Waterproof membrane A flexible rubberlike material used in tiled tub and shower installations, and also in thickset counter installations.

Zero clearance Term that applies to prefab fireplace units that can be installed next to framing and other combustible materials.

INDEX

PHOTO CREDITS

All photography by John Parsekian/CH, unless otherwise noted.

page 1: Mark Samu, design: Lucianna Samu Design **page 2:** Mark Lohman **pages 6–7:** *both* Mark Lohman **pages 8–9:** *main* Mark Lohman; *tile insets:* courtesy of Abbate Tile **pages 10–11:** *main* Mark Samu; *tile insets* courtesy of Abbate Tile **page 13:** *top right* ME Jordan/Bruce Coleman, Inc.; *bottom* JC Carton/Carto/Bruce Coleman, Inc.; *top left* Phillip H. Ennis Photography **page 14:** courtesy of American Olean **page 15:** *top* Brian Vanden Brink; *center both* courtesy of Abbate Tile; *bottom both* David Phelps **page 18:** *left* Mark Lohman; *right* Jessie Walker, architect: Lenore Weiss Baigelman, Full Circle Architects **page 19:** *bottom right & top* Jessie Walker; *bottom left* Mark Samu, architect: Bruce Nagle, AIA **page 20:** Phillip H. Ennis Photography, design: Anne Cooper Interiors **page 21:** *top right* Anne Gummerson; *bottom right* Phillip H. Ennis Photography, design: Amir Ilin, Kuche Cuchina; *bottom left* Mark Samu, architect: Andy Levtovsky, AIA; *top left* davidduncanlivingston.com **page 22:** *left* Brian Vanden Brink; *right* Stickley Photo•Graphic **page 23:** *top right* Mark Samu, design: Lucianna Samu Design; *bottom* Brian Vanden Brink; *top left* Phillip H. Ennis Photography **page 24:** Phillip H. Ennis Photography, design: Diane Lowenthal, Lowenthal & Partners **page 25:** *top* Stickley Photo•Graphic; *bottom right* Mark Samu, stylist: Tia Burns; *bottom left* Jessie Walker, design: Dave Hagerman **page 26:** *bottom left* Brian Vanden Brink; *bottom right* Jessie Walker, design: Dave McFadden, Past Basket Cabinetry **page 27:** *top right* Tony Giammarino/Giammarino & Dworkin; *bottom* Phillip H. Ennis Photography, architect: Opacic Architects; *top left* Mark Lohman **page 28:** *left* Mark Lohman; *right* Phillip H. Ennis Photography, design: Salem Hill Studios **page 29:** *top* Stickley Photo•Graphic, design: Pratt & Larson Tile & Stone; *bottom right* Tony Giammarino/Giammarino & Dworkin, builder: Sue Kipp Construction; *bottom left* Tony Giammarino/Giammarino & Dworkin, design Marge Thomas **pages 30–31:** *all* Mark Lohman **page 32:** Phillip H. Ennis Photography, design: Stephanie Wolf, M&S

Associates **page 33:** *top right & bottom right* Phillip H. Ennis Photography; *bottom left* Mark Samu/courtesy of Hearst Magazines; *top left* Eric Roth **pages 56–57:** *main* Peter Tata, design Cindy Cook/Interior Selections **page 58:** *both* courtesy of Abbate Tile **page 59:** davidduncanlivingston.com **page 60:** courtesy of American Olean **page 61:** *top* Phillip H. Ennis Photography; *bottom* courtesy of Abbate Tile **page 66:** courtesy of Abbate Tile **page 75:** *bottom right* courtesy of American Olean **pages 78–81:** *all* Neal Barrett **page 82:** *top right* Jessie Walker, architect: Lenore Baigelman, Full Circle Architects; *bottom right & bottom left* Tony Giammarino/Giammarino & Dworkin; *top left* Mark Samu/courtesy of Hearst Magazines **page 83:** Stickley Photo•Graphic **page 84:** *top right* Mark Samu; *bottom left* melabee m miller, design: Camille Waldron; *top left* melabee m miller, design: Mock Fox Interiors **page 85:** Brian Vanden Brink **pages 86–87:** Mark Samu, architect: Montllor Box, AIA **page 88:** courtesy of Maticad **page 89:** *top* courtesy of DalTile; *bottom both* courtesy of Maticad **page 92:** courtesy of DalTile **pages 94–97:** *all* Merle Henkenius **page 104:** *top* Jessie Walker, design: Arlene Semel; *bottom* Peter Tata, design: James Carroll **page 105:** *top right & bottom right* Mark Lohman; *bottom left* Tony Giammarino/Giammarino & Dworkin; *top left* Stickley Photo•Graphic **page 106:** *left* Phillip H. Ennis Photography, architect: Elizabeth Steimberg; *right* davidduncanlivingston.com **page 107:** *top right* Tria Giovan; *bottom* Stickley Photo•Graphic, design: Shelburne Development; *top left* Stickley Photo•Graphic **page 108–109:** Bradley Olman; *tile insets* courtesy of Fraser Clay Works, Inc. **page 110:** courtesy of American Olean **page 125:** *top* Beth Singer **pages 126–127:** *all* Neal Barrett/CH **page 128:** Mark Lohman **page 129:** *top right* Mark Samu, design: Sherrill Canet Design; *bottom* Mark Lohman; *top left* Tony Giammarino/Giammarino & Dworkin **page 130:** *right* Mark Lohman; *bottom left* Ivy Moriber-Neal/Ivy D Photography; *top left* Tony Giammarino/Giammarino & Dworkin **page 131:** Stickley Photo•Graphic, design: O'Leal & Associates **pages 132–133:** Mark Lohman; *tile insets* courtesy of Motawi TileWorks

page 137: courtesy of American Olean **page 139:** *top* courtesy of Spain Tile **page 142:** Tria Giovan **page 145:** courtesy of DalTile **page 152:** *right* courtesy of Artistic Tile, Hamptons Blend; *bottom left* Tony Giammarino/Giammarino & Dworkin; *top left* courtesy of Artistic Tile, Geometrica **page 154:** melabee m miller, design Deck House, LLC **page 155:** *top right* Mark Samu, design: Kitchens by Ken Kelly; *bottom right* Brian Vanden Brink; *bottom left* Roger Turk, design: Showplace Design & Remodeling; *top left* Mark Samu, design: Durst Construction **pages 156–157:** *main* Brian Vanden Brink; *tile insets* courtesy of Motawi Tile **page 158:** courtesy of DalTile **page 161:** *top* courtesy of Tile Restoration Center **page 164:** K. Rice/H. Armstrong Roberts **page 166:** Grey Crawford **page 168:** *right* Mark Lohman; *bottom left* Tony Giammarino/Giammarino & Dworkin; *bottom right* Mark Samu, builder: Access Builders **page 169:** Stickley Photo•Graphic **page 170:** Stickley Photo•Graphic, design: Pratt & Larson Tile & Stone **page 171:** *top right* melabee m miller, design: Karen Shapiro; *bottom right* Tony Giammarino/Giammarino & Dworkin; *left* Stickley Photo•Graphic **pages 172–173:** *main* Tria Giovan; *tile insets* courtesy of Motawi TileWorks **page 174:** Jessie Walker **page 177:** *bottom left* Crandall & Crandall; *bottom right* courtesy of American Olean **page 183:** courtesy of Inma Roca Associates **page 184:** Mark Lohman **page 185:** *top right & top left* Stickley Photo•Graphic; *bottom right* Mark Lohman; *bottom right* Jerry Pavia, design: Irina & Erik Gronborg **pages 186–187:** *all* Brian Vanden Brink **pages 188–189:** *main* Phillip H. Ennis Photography, design: Christina Van Cleef; *tile insets* courtesy of Motawi TileWorks **page 193:** courtesy of American Olean **pages 200–201:** *main* Anne Gummerson, architect: Virginia Navid; *tile insets* courtesy of Abbate Tile **page 202:** Jerry Pavia **page 204:** Mark Lohman **page 206:** Bradley Olman **page 208:** Roger Turk **page 212:** *bottom* courtesy of American Olean **page 213:** *top* courtesy of DalTile **page 214:** *top* courtesy of DalTile **page 215:** *top* courtesy of American Olean **page 216:** Abbate Tile **page 217:** Eric Roth **back cover** *top* Mark Lohman; *bottom left & bottom center* Neal Barrett/CH

Have a home improvement, decorating, or gardening project? Look for these and other fine Creative Homeowner books wherever books are sold.

Transform a room with trimwork.
Over 550 photos and illustrations.
240 pp.; 8¹/₂" × 10⁷/₈"
BOOK #: 277500

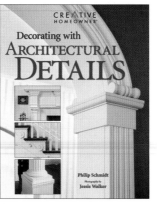

Classic home design treatments.
Over 350 photos and illustrations.
224 pp.; 8¹/₂" × 10⁷/₈"
BOOK #: 278225

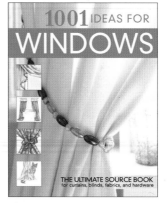

Comprehensive guide to window
treatments. Over 1,000 photos
and illos. 240 pp.; 8¹/₂" × 10⁷/₈"
BOOK #: 279408

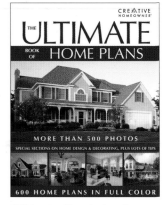

600 best-selling designs from
leading architects. Over 500
color photos. 528 pp.; 8¹/₂" × 11"
BOOK #: 277039

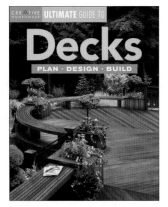

How to improve your home by
adding a deck. Over 750 photos
and illos. 288 pp.; 8¹/₂" × 10⁷/₈"
BOOK #: 277168

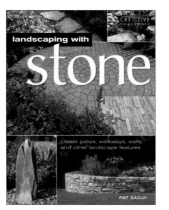

Ideas for incorporating stone into
the landscape. Over 400 color photos and illos. 224 pp.; 8¹/₂" × 10⁷/₈"
BOOK #: 274172

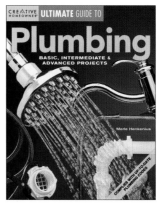

Take the guesswork out of plumbing
repair. More than 750 photos and
illustrations. 272 pp.; 8¹/₂" × 10⁷/₈"
BOOK #: 278210

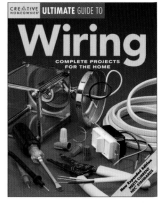

Best-selling house-wiring manual.
Over 925 color photos and illus-
trations. 288 pp.; 8¹/₂" × 10⁷/₈"
BOOK #: 278237

Complete guide to decorative
paint techniques. Over 300
photos. 240 pp.; 8¹/₂" × 10⁷/₈"
BOOK #: 279020

How to work with space, color,
pattern, texture. Over 440 photos. 288 pp.; 9" × 10"
BOOK #: 279672

Impressive guide to garden design
and plant selection. More than 950
photos and illos. 384 pp.; 9" × 10"
BOOK #: 274610

Lavishly illustrated with portraits of
over 100 flowering plants; more
than 500 photos. 208 pp.; 9" × 10"
BOOK #: 274032

For more information and to place an order, go to **www.creativehomeowner.com**